SPOOKY
FOOD

WHIMSICAL TREATS

SPOOKY FOOD

FUN HALLOWEEN RECIPES for Ghosts, Ghouls, Vampires, Jack-o-Lanterns, Witches, Zombies, and More

CAYLA GALLAGHER

Skyhorse Publishing

Skyhorse Publishing books may be purchased in bulk at special discounts for sales promotion, corporate gifts, fund-raising, or educational purposes. Special editions can also be created to specifications. For details, contact the Special Sales Department, Skyhorse Publishing, 307 West 36th Street, 11th Floor, New York, NY 10018 or info@skyhorsepublishing.com.

Skyhorse® and Skyhorse Publishing® are registered trademarks of Skyhorse Publishing, Inc.®, a Delaware corporation.

Visit our website at www.skyhorsepublishing.com.

10 9 8 7 6 5 4 3 2 1

Library of Congress Cataloging-in-Publication Data

Names: Gallagher, Cayla, author.
Title: Spooky food: 80 fun Halloween recipes for ghosts, ghouls, vampires, jack-o-lanterns, witches, zombies, and more / Cayla Gallagher.
Description: New York, NY: Skyhorse Publishing, [2021] | Series: Whimsical treats | Includes index. | Identifiers: LCCN 2021006898 (print) | LCCN 2021006899 (ebook) | ISBN 9781510759534 (print) | ISBN 9781510759541 (Ebook)
Subjects: LCSH: Halloween cooking. | LCGFT: Cookbooks.
Classification: LCC TX739.2.H34 G35 2021 (print) | LCC TX739.2.H34 (ebook) | DDC 641.5/68—dc23
LC record available at https://lccn.loc.gov/2021006898
LC ebook record available at https://lccn.loc.gov/2021006899

Cover design by Daniel Brount
Cover photos by Cayla Gallagher

Print ISBN: 978-1-5107-5953-4
Ebook ISBN: 978-1-5107-5954-1

Printed in China

CONTENTS

Black Poison Apples, page 135

Black Widow Cupcakes, page 13

INTRODUCTION

I am so excited to welcome you to my fifth cookbook, *Spooky Food*! Halloween is such a fun holiday, and I love the endless variety of sweets and treats. In this book I've compiled my favorite recipes from previous years, as well as some brand-new recipes that are sure to please both your sweet and spooky tooth!

Hosting a fun costume party? Try out my Rainbow Candy Apples (page 137) or Rose Gold Skull Cake (page 47). For a unique twist to a Halloween cake, I recommend my Pink Lemonade Halloween Cake (page 41). We're using my grandmother's famous lemon cake recipe, and it is the perfect balance of tart and sweet.

If you're planning a night of ghost hunting and séances in your basement, how about trying my Oujia Board Sheet Cake (page 45) and Marshmallow Ghosts (page 107)? Just make sure to end the séance before you break for cake—you don't want any ghosts hanging around in your kitchen! Although if they help clean the dishes, maybe it won't be so bad.

For my readers who appreciate the gorier side of Halloween, I recommend my Blood Clot Lollipops (page 119), Bleeding Heart Panna Cotta (page 115), and Blood Bag Drinks (page 159). These recipes look so creepy and cool! When choosing which red food coloring to use, I recommend using Crimson in the Color Right food coloring set by Wilton, which is several shades deeper than traditional red food coloring. If you don't have access to this specific brand, add the *tiniest* touch of blue food coloring (about $\frac{1}{12}$ of a drop) along with your red food coloring. This will deepen the red and make it look closer to blood, but isn't enough to dye your mixture purple.

I also want to give a *massive* thank-you to each and every one of you. I feel so incredibly lucky to have had the opportunity to turn my recipes into published cookbooks and I still pinch myself when I see them on store shelves. I wouldn't be here without the support of each and every one of you and I hope that you know just how much I appreciate it. I hope you enjoy my books and if you ever have any questions about my recipes, feel free to reach out to me on social media, and I'll do my best to help!

Happy haunted baking!

Cakes & Cupcakes

Cauldron Cupcakes with Gooey Centers

MAKES 12 CUPCAKES

These cupcakes are baked in cauldron-shaped silicone cupcake cups, which I absolutely love! I kept them in the cups after baking, and when combined with the gooey, chocolaty center, they become the perfect mini cake to eat with a spoon.

Cupcake Batter:
1 cup unsalted butter, room temperature
2 cups sugar
1 teaspoon vanilla extract
6 eggs, room temperature
3 cups all-purpose flour
1 teaspoon baking soda
1 teaspoon salt
½ cup cocoa powder
1¼ cups buttermilk
1 cup chocolate chips
24 chocolate squares (from any chocolate bar—I used Lindt, so each square was about 1 inch)

Buttercream:
2 cups unsalted butter, room temperature
1½ teaspoons vanilla extract
5 cups confectioners' sugar
Red and orange food coloring

Decoration:
Mini marshmallows
Skull candies
Candy eyeballs

Bake the Cupcakes:
1. Preheat oven to 350°F. Beat the butter and sugar with an electric mixer until light and fluffy. Add the vanilla and eggs, one at a time, beating with each addition.

2. In a separate bowl, combine the flour, baking soda, salt, and cocoa powder. Add this to the butter mixture in 2 additions, alternating with the buttermilk. Add the chocolate chips and mix well.

3. Pour the batter into 12 silicone cauldron molds. Stick 2 chocolate squares into the center of each.

4. Bake for 20 minutes, then cool completely.

Make the Buttercream:
1. Beat the butter with an electric mixer until pale and fluffy. Add the vanilla and mix well. Add the confectioners' sugar 1 cup at a time, then beat for 3 to 5 minutes, until fluffy.

2. Dye the buttercream orange. Then add several drops of red food coloring and fold until it is swirled throughout the buttercream.

3. Place the buttercream in a piping bag fitted with a large, round piping tip.

To Decorate:
1. Pipe dollops of buttercream onto the cupcakes to look like bubbling cauldrons.

2. Decorate with some mini marshmallows, skull candies, and candy eyeballs.

Brain Cupcakes

MAKES ABOUT 18 CUPCAKES

These vanilla cupcakes are filled with strawberry jam to give you an ooey, gooey, brain-eating experience!

Cupcake Batter:
1 cup unsalted butter, room temperature
2 cups sugar
3 teaspoons vanilla extract
6 large eggs
3 cups all-purpose flour
1 teaspoon baking soda
1 teaspoon salt
1½ cups sour cream
Red food coloring

Buttercream:
3 cups unsalted butter, room temperature
1½ teaspoons vanilla extract
7 cups confectioners' sugar
Pink food coloring

Extra:
½ cup strawberry jam

Bake the Cupcakes:

1. Preheat the oven to 350°F and line a cupcake pan with liners.

2. Beat the butter and sugar with an electric mixer until pale and smooth. Add the vanilla and eggs, one at a time, mixing with each addition.

3. In a separate bowl, combine the flour, baking soda, and salt. Add this to the batter in 2 additions, alternating with the sour cream. Use a few drops of food coloring to dye the batter red.

4. Spoon the batter into your prepared cupcake pan. Bake for 20 to 25 minutes, or until a skewer inserted into the centers comes out clean. Cool completely.

Make the Buttercream:

1. Beat the butter with an electric mixer until pale and fluffy. Add the vanilla and mix until combined. Add the confectioners' sugar 1 cup at a time, mixing with each addition. Then beat for 3 to 5 minutes, until fluffy.

2. Dye the buttercream pale pink with just a bit of food coloring. Place in a piping bag fitted with a large, round piping tip.

To Decorate:

1. Use the wide end of a piping tip to cut holes into the centers of the cupcakes. Fill the holes with strawberry jam.

2. To create the brain pattern, pipe 2 lines of buttercream across the centers of the cupcakes, then pipe squiggles on either side. Enjoy!

Glow-in-the-Dark Cupcakes

MAKES 24 CUPCAKES

Tonic water is such a fun ingredient to use during Halloween, because when set under a black light, it glows in the dark! This recipe combines tonic water with Jell-O as a fun coating for cupcakes. Then just turn off your lights and switch on the black light to see your cupcakes glow!

1 cup unsalted butter, room temperature
1¼ cup + 1 tablespoon tonic water
6 cups confectioners' sugar
3-ounce packet of Jell-O (yellow or green works best)
1 cup boiling water
24 cupcakes, any flavor, chilled

1. Place the butter in a large bowl and beat with an electric mixer until pale and fluffy. Add ¼ cup and 1 tablespoon tonic water and 4 cups confectioners sugar and mix until combined. Add the remaining 2 cups confectioners' sugar and beat well.

2. Place the buttercream in a piping bag fitted with a large, round tip. Pipe a large swirl of buttercream onto each cupcake. Transfer the cupcakes to the refrigerator for at least an hour, until the buttercream is very stiff.

3. In the meantime, make the glaze. Combine the Jell-O and boiling water and whisk until the powder has fully dissolved. Add 1 cup chilled tonic water and whisk. Allow to cool to room temperature, but not so cool that it starts to set.

4. Dunk the chilled cupcakes into the glaze so that only the buttercream is getting coated. Alternatively, you can brush the glaze onto the cupcakes with a pastry brush. Place the cupcakes in the freezer until the glaze has set, about 10 to 15 minutes, then repeat 5 more times for a total of 6 layers of glaze—this will make the cupcakes glow the brightest!

5. Serve the cupcakes under a black light and watch them glow!

Pumpkin Spice Cupcakes

MAKES 12 CUPCAKES

I fall back (pun intended) on this pumpkin cake recipe every time I want to bake something that tastes like the autumn. The pumpkin keeps this cake moist and so incredibly succulent. The variety of spices can be substituted with 2 teaspoons pumpkin pie spice, if you have a premixed version on hand. If you'd like to kick it up a notch, add 2 tablespoons instant coffee powder to the cake batter—it makes it even more luxurious.

Cupcakes:
2 large eggs
1½ cups sugar
15 ounces plain pumpkin puree
½ cup unsalted butter, melted
2½ cups all-purpose flour
2 teaspoons baking soda
½ teaspoon salt
1½ teaspoons cinnamon
¾ teaspoon ground ginger
½ teaspoon nutmeg
⅛ teaspoon allspice
⅛ teaspoon cloves

Buttercream:
2 cups unsalted butter, room temperature
¼ cup canned plain pumpkin
½ teaspoon pumpkin pie spice (or use the
   mixture above)
1 teaspoon vanilla extract
5 cups confectioners' sugar
Orange food coloring

Decoration:
Leaf sprinkles
Candy pumpkins

Bake the Cupcakes:
1. Preheat the oven to 350°F and line a cupcake pan with paper liners.

2. Combine the eggs, sugar, pumpkin puree, and butter in a large bowl. In a separate bowl, combine the flour, baking soda, salt, cinnamon, ginger, nutmeg, allspice, and cloves. Add this to the pumpkin mixture and mix well.

3. Divide the batter into your prepared pan and bake for 20 to 25 minutes, or until a skewer inserted into the center comes out clean.

Make the Buttercream:
1. Beat the butter, canned pumpkin, and pumpkin pie spice with an electric mixer until fluffy. Add the vanilla and mix well. Add the confectioners' sugar 1 cup at a time, beating with each addition. Add a couple drops of orange food coloring and beat for 3 to 5 minutes, until fluffy.

2. Place the buttercream in a piping bag fitted with a large star-shaped piping tip.

Assembly:
1. Pipe swirls of buttercream onto the cupcakes. Decorate with leaf sprinkles and candy pumpkins. Enjoy!

CHOCOLATE PUMPKIN CUPCAKES

MAKES 24 CUPCAKES

These cupcakes have a chocolate pumpkin cake base and are topped with pumpkin cream cheese frosting. Pumpkin and chocolate taste delicious together, especially with this life-changing cream cheese frosting. Smooth, creamy, and just like pumpkin cheesecake!

Cupcake Batter:
2 cups all-purpose flour
2 cups sugar
¾ cup cocoa powder
2 teaspoons pumpkin pie spice
2 teaspoons baking powder
1½ teaspoons baking soda
1 teaspoon salt
1 cup milk
½ cup vegetable oil
2 large eggs
2 teaspoons vanilla extract
½ cup canned pure pumpkin
1 cup boiling water

Pumpkin Cream Cheese Frosting:
1½ cups unsalted butter, room
    temperature
8 ounces cream cheese, room
    temperature
½ cup canned pure pumpkin
1 teaspoon vanilla extract
1 teaspoon pumpkin pie spice
3 cups confectioners' sugar
Orange food coloring
12 Pumpkin Cake Pops (page 75)

Bake the Cupcakes:

1. Preheat the oven to 350°F and line 2 cupcake pans with cupcake liners.

2. Place the flour, sugar, cocoa powder, pumpkin pie spice, baking powder, baking soda, and salt in a large bowl and mix.

3. Add the milk, vegetable oil, eggs, vanilla, and canned pumpkin and mix with an electric mixer until combined.

4. Slowly add the boiling water and mix until well combined.

5. Divide the batter evenly between your prepared pans and bake for 15 to 20 minutes, until a skewer inserted into the center comes out clean. Cool for 15 minutes in the pan, then turn onto a wire rack and cool completely.

Make the Frosting:

1. Beat the butter, cream cheese, and canned pumpkin with an electric mixer until fluffy. Add the vanilla and pumpkin pie spice and combine.

2. Add the confectioners' sugar and beat until light and fluffy.

3. Dye the frosting your desired shade of orange, then place in a piping bag fitted with a 2D star-shaped piping tip.

To Decorate:

1. Top the cupcakes with a swirl of buttercream.

2. Place a Pumpkin Cake Pop on top and enjoy!

Black Widow Cupcakes

MAKES 12 CUPCAKES

These cupcakes use several fun techniques that result in a showstopping cupcake that will surely impress your friends! We are dipping the cupcakes in hard-crack chocolate shell, which will give the frosting a glossy look and contrast beautifully with the delicious vanilla buttercream underneath. Then we're using the trendy marshmallow spiderweb technique to easily create realistic cobwebs that wrap around the cupcakes.

Cupcakes:
1 cup all-purpose flour
1 cup sugar
½ cup cocoa powder
1 teaspoon baking powder
¾ teaspoon baking soda
½ teaspoon salt
½ cup milk
¼ cup vegetable oil
1 large egg
1 teaspoon vanilla extract
½ cup boiling water
½ cup chocolate chips
Plain Buttercream (page 3)

Chocolate Coating:
12 ounces milk chocolate
¼ cup coconut oil, melted

Decoration:
½ cup black fondant
¼ cup red fondant
¼ cup long black sprinkles
1 cup mini marshmallows

Bake the Cupcakes:
1. Preheat the oven to 350°F and line a cupcake pan with paper liners.

2. Place the flour, sugar, cocoa powder, baking powder, baking soda, and salt in a large bowl and mix.

3. Add the milk, vegetable oil, egg, and vanilla and mix with an electric mixer until combined.

4. Slowly add the boiling water and mix until well combined. Add the chocolate chips and mix well.

5. Divide the batter evenly into your prepared pan and bake for 30 to 35 minutes, until a skewer inserted into the center comes out clean. Cool completely.

6. Spoon the buttercream into a piping bag fitted with a large, round piping tip. Pipe swirls onto the cupcakes, then place the cupcakes in the refrigerator while you make the decorations. The chocolate coating will need a cold surface in order to harden, so we need the cupcakes to be a little chilled.

Make the Chocolate Coating:
1. Place the milk chocolate in a microwave-safe bowl and microwave for 30-second intervals until melted, stirring at each interval. Add the coconut oil to the melted chocolate and mix until fully incorporated.

(Continued on next page)

2. Dunk each cupcake upside down into the chocolate coating, allow the excess to drip off, then place it upright on your work surface. The chocolate coating will stiffen before your eyes!

3. Return the cupcakes to the refrigerator while you make the decorations.

Make the Decorations:

1. Roll the black fondant into little balls of varying sizes for your spider bodies. Shape the red fondant into small triangles—you'll need 2 triangles per spider. Stick 2 triangles onto each spider to create an hourglass shape. If the triangles aren't sticking, wet your finger and dab it onto the spider!

2. Stick the black sprinkles into the sides of the spiders so each one has 8 legs. Set the spiders aside on a plate lined with plastic wrap.

3. Place the marshmallows in a microwave-safe bowl and heat for 30 seconds, until melted.

4. Put on some latex gloves, then dip them in the marshmallow. Press your hands together, then pull them apart to see the marshmallow look like spiderwebs. Gently wrap the marshmallow around the cupcakes.

5. Stick the fondant spiders to the sticky web and serve!

Slithering Snake Cupcakes

MAKES 12 CUPCAKES

I wanted to include a unique flavor in this book—cinnamon raisin! These are the perfect breakfast cupcake (if that was an actual thing), as they don't taste too sweet and are topped with a swirl of delicious cinnamon cream cheese frosting. Not a fan of raisins? Simply omit and enjoy the cinnamon flavors on their own!

Cupcake Batter:
½ cup unsalted butter, room temperature
1 cup sugar
2 teaspoons vanilla extract
3 large eggs
1½ cups all-purpose flour
½ teaspoon baking soda
½ teaspoon salt
2–3 teaspoons cinnamon
¾ cup sour cream
1 cup raisins

Frosting:
1½ cups unsalted butter, room temperature
9 ounces cream cheese, room temperature
2 teaspoons vanilla extract
3 teaspoons cinnamon
3 cups confectioners' sugar
Red and orange food coloring

Decoration:
¾ cup orange fondant
1 tablespoon each red, black, and blue fondant
1 tablespoon black sprinkles

Bake the Cupcakes:

1. Preheat oven to 350°F and line a cupcake pan with paper liners.

2. Beat the butter and sugar with an electric mixer until smooth. Add vanilla and eggs, one at a time, mixing with each addition.

3. In a separate bowl, combine the flour, baking soda, salt, and cinnamon. Add this to the batter in 2 additions, alternating with the sour cream. Add the raisins and fold to combine.

4. Spoon the batter into your prepared pan and bake for 15 to 20 minutes, or until a skewer inserted into the centers comes out clean. Cool completely.

Make the Frosting:

1. Beat the butter and cream cheese with an electric mixer until fluffy. Add vanilla and cinnamon and combine. Add the confectioners' sugar and beat until light and fluffy.

2. Prepare a piping bag fitted with a large round piping tip. Use a clean brush to paint vertical stripes of the red and orange food coloring onto the insides of the bag. Gently spoon the buttercream into the piping bag. You'll see colorful stripes appear onto the sides! Squeeze buttercream back into the bowl until you begin to see the stripes appear in the piped buttercream.

(Continued on page 17)

Assembly:

1. Divide the orange into 12 pieces, then roll into 3- to 4-inch-long ropes. Use the black and blue fondant to create markings on the snakes and the red as their tongues. Use the black sprinkles as the snakes' eyes. If you are having trouble with the fondant sticking together, wet your finger and use as glue to attach the markings to the snakes.

2. Pipe swirls of buttercream onto each cupcake. Top with a snake and enjoy!

Halloween Cupcakes 6 Ways

No matter your Halloween style, one of these cupcakes is sure to please!

6 cupcakes (any recipe)
Plain Buttercream (page 3)
Food Coloring
Piping bags
Piping tips
Festive candy and sprinkles

Pumpkin:

1. Using a large, round piping tip, pipe a large dollop of orange buttercream into the center of the cupcake. Then pipe vertical stripes, starting from the base of the dollop and working toward the top.

2. Using a small, round piping tip, pipe the pumpkin's stem and vine with brown buttercream.

Halloween Unicorn:

1. Cover the entire surface with black buttercream.

2. Place a piping bag fitted with the star-shaped piping tip into a tall glass. Spread 4 vertical stripes of black buttercream onto the insides, evenly spacing them apart. Spread the pink buttercream into one open space and repeat with the yellow, green, and purple. Squeeze enough buttercream out of the tip until all 5 colors come out.

3. Pipe swirls to create the mane, with a large dollop in the center where the horn will go.

4. Pipe the ears with the black buttercream. Use a small, round piping tip to make the inner ears with pink buttercream and eyes with white.

5. Insert a birthday candle into the large dollop of buttercream at the beginning of the mane.

Creepy Monster:

1. Fit a piping bag with the large, round piping tip. Spread purple and green buttercream both vertically into the same piping bag, so that one side is green and one side is purple. Pipe a little bit on the plate until you see both colors appear.

2. Pipe a swirl of buttercream onto the cupcake.

3. Decorate with candy eyes and round white candies.

Candy Corn:

1. Using a large, round piping tip, pipe a large circle of yellow buttercream onto the cupcake.

2. Using the same piping tip but with orange buttercream, pipe a smaller circle on top.

3. Using the same piping tip but with white buttercream, pipe a dollop on the top.

Gory Wound:

1. Cut a crater out the center of the cupcake, making it the shape you'd like your wound to be.

2. Line the inside of the crater and coat the entire surface of the cupcake in a generous layer of plain buttercream.

3. Fill the wound with strawberry jam.

4. Use a small, round piping tip to pipe stitches across the wound with the black buttercream.

Black Cat:

1. Using a small, star-shaped piping tip, pipe black fur all over the cupcake. Make larger dollops for the ears and nose. Use a medium, round piping tip to pipe eyes with yellow buttercream.

2. Use a small, round piping tip to create the inner ears and nose with pink buttercream and pupils and mouth with black buttercream.

Poison Apple Cake

Spooky but also delicious with the addition of a caramel apple on top! Too bloody-looking for your taste? Simply use a different color of food coloring for the ganache drip! This is my favorite cake recipe, but with the addition of fresh apples in the cake batter and apple butter and jelly in the frosting, to give it a seasonal touch.

Cake:

1 cup unsalted butter, room temperature

2 cups sugar

3 teaspoons vanilla extract

6 large eggs

3 cups all-purpose flour

1 teaspoon baking soda

1 teaspoon salt

1½ cups sour cream

2 apples, finely chopped

Wilton cinnamon graham flavoring
   (or 1 teaspoon cinnamon)

Red food coloring

Plain Buttercream (page 3)

2 tablespoons apple butter

¼ cup apple jelly (or apple juice), warm

Caramel Apple:

1 caramel apple (page 133)

White candy melts, melted

Red Ganache Drip:

5 ounces high quality white chocolate

2 ounces whipping cream, hot

Red food coloring

Bake the Cake:

1. Preheat oven to 350°F and grease and flour 4 (6-inch) round cake pans.

2. Beat the butter and sugar with an electric mixer until pale and smooth. Add the vanilla and eggs, one at a time, mixing with each addition.

3. In a separate bowl, combine the flour, baking soda, and salt. Add this to the batter in 2 additions, alternating with the sour cream. Add the apples, cinnamon, and 3 or 4 dops red food coloring, and mix to combine.

4. Spoon the batter into your prepared pans and bake for 30 minutes, or until a skewer inserted into the centers comes out clean. Cool completely.

5. Measure 1½ cups of buttercream and mix in the apple butter. This buttercream will be used for spreading between the cake layers.

Assembly:

1. Slice the tops and bottoms off the cakes to smooth the surface and remove any excess browning. Stack the cakes, brushing each layer with the warm apple jelly and spreading the apple butter buttercream on top before adding the next layer.

(Continued on next page)

2. Once chilled, coat the cake in a thin layer of the remaining buttercream, which will catch any excess cake crumbs. Chill the cake in the refrigerator for 20 minutes. Once chilled, coat the cake in a thick, generous layer of buttercream. Set in the refrigerator to chill while you make the apple decoration.

3. Dunk the caramel apple in the white candy melts and place on a square of parchment paper. Place the apple in the refrigerator for the candy melts to stiffen. You may need to do 2 coats.

Make the Ganache:
1. Combine the white chocolate and whipping cream in a bowl. Whisk until fully incorporated, then add 5 to 6 drops of the red food coloring, until the ganache is your desired shade of red.

2. Pour some onto the top of the cake and smooth over the surface with a knife, pushing it off the edges of the cake to create a drip pattern.

3. Place the apple on top of the cake. Cut eyes and nose shapes out of parchment paper, brush them with corn syrup, and stick them to the apple.

4. Spoon the red ganache drip on top of the apple, pressing the parchment paper to the apple to make sure ganache doesn't get in through the sides.

5. Allow the ganache to stiffen for about 30 minutes, then carefully remove the parchment paper with tweezers and enjoy!

Brainy Fault Line Cake

MAKES A 6-INCH CAKE

The trendy fault line cake has taken a spooky turn and is filled with brains! This technique not only looks super impressive—it's actually quite easy as well!

Cake:

1 cup unsalted butter, room temperature
2 cups sugar
3 teaspoons vanilla extract
6 large eggs
3 cups all-purpose flour
1 teaspoon baking soda
1 teaspoon salt
1½ cups sour cream
Red food coloring
1 cup chocolate chips
½ teaspoon activated charcoal powder or
    black food coloring (see page 29 for
    more information)
1½ cups chocolate hazelnut spread
Plain Buttercream (page 3)
Brown, yellow, pink, and red food coloring

Blood Ganache:

½ cup white chocolate chips
¼ cup whipping cream

Bake the Cake:

1. Preheat oven to 350°F and grease and flour 3 (6-inch) round cake pans.

2. Beat the butter and sugar with an electric mixer until pale and smooth. Add the vanilla and eggs, one at a time, mixing with each addition.

3. In a separate bowl, combine the flour, baking soda, and salt. Add this to the batter in 2 additions, alternating with the sour cream.

4. Divide the batter between 2 bowls. Dye one bowl red using a few drops of food coloring, and stir in the chocolate chips. To the other bowl, add the charcoal powder and chocolate hazelnut spread.

5. Dollop both the red and brown batter into your prepared cake pans. This will create multicolored cake! Bake for 30-40 minutes, or until a skewer inserted into the centers comes out clean. Cool completely.

6. Remove ⅓ of the buttercream to a separate bowl and dye it pale pink using just a couple drops of food coloring. Dye the remaining buttercream a beige color—use both brown and yellow food coloring to create your desired shade (adding a bit of yellow food coloring adds a warm, peachy touch when mixed with the brown).

(Continued on page 27)

Assembly:

1. Slice the tops and bottoms off the cakes to smooth the surface and remove any excess browning. Use a 4-inch round cookie cutter to cut the center out of one of the cakes. We'll use the smaller circle, but save the cake scraps for later in this recipe.

2. Place one of the larger cakes onto your work surface and cover it in a generous coating of the beige-colored buttercream. Place it in the refrigerator for chill for 20 minutes. Place the smaller 4-inch cake on top and coat in a thin layer of pink buttercream. Place the remaining large cake on top and coat in a thin layer of beige buttercream. Stick 3 bubble tea straws (or regular straws, but these will be thicker and more supportive) into the center of the cake to stabilize it. Trim them so that they're flush with the top of the cake. Place the cake in the refrigerator to chill for 20 minutes. Then carefully cover the top layer in a generous coating of beige buttercream.

3. Use a food-safe paintbrush and red food coloring to paint vertical stripes onto the inside of a piping bag. Spoon the pink buttercream into the bag and snip a hole at the end to create a large, round piping tip. Pipe the brain pattern into the middle space between the two layers.

4. Place some of the cake scraps and a couple dollops of buttercream into a bowl and mix with an electric mixer Form the mixture into an oval-shaped dome and place on the top of the cake. Pipe on a brain pattern with the remaining pink buttercream. Start with 2 long stripes down the center, then squiggles on each side of the brain.

5. Use the same food-safe paintbrush to dab red food coloring directly onto the cake to resemble cuts and bruises.

6. And finally, the ganache! Place the white chocolate in a microwave-safe bowl and microwave for 30-second intervals, until fully melted. Add the whipping cream and mix until fully combined. Add some red food coloring and mix well. Place the ganache into a piping bag or a syringe with a medium-size piping tip. Pipe blood all over the cake! Then serve and enjoy your edible brains!

Blackest Black Cake

MAKES A 6-INCH CAKE

This is the spookiest cake you'll find, because it's jet black without using any food coloring! We're using activated charcoal powder, which is incredibly pigmented so a little goes a very long way. Be sure to choose the edible/food-safe version. Charcoal powder is also used in medicine to absorb toxins in the stomach, so if you take any medication, be sure to check with your doctor first. If you have any worries, you can simply replace the charcoal powder with black food coloring!

Cake Batter:
2 cups all-purpose flour
2 cups sugar
¾ cup cocoa powder + extra for coating the pan
2 teaspoons baking powder
1½ teaspoons baking soda
1 tablespoon activated charcoal powder
1 teaspoon salt
1 cup milk
½ cup vegetable oil
2 large eggs
2 teaspoons vanilla extract
1 cup boiling water

Decoration:
Plain Buttercream (page 3)
1 tablespoon activated charcoal powder
Black sugar
Black sprinkles

Bake the Cake:

1. Preheat oven to 350°F and grease and flour 3 (6-inch) round baking pans.

2. Place the flour, sugar, cocoa powder, baking powder, baking soda, charcoal powder, and salt in a large bowl and mix.

3. Add the milk, vegetable oil, eggs, and vanilla and mix with an electric mixer until combined. Slowly add the boiling water and mix until well combined.

4. Divide the batter evenly between the pans and bake for 30 to 35 minutes, until a skewer inserted into the center comes out clean. Cool for 15 minutes in the pan, then turn onto a wire rack and cool completely.

Assembly:

1. Beat the buttercream with the charcoal powder until fully combined.

2. Slice the tops and bottoms off the cakes to smooth the surface and remove any excess browning. Stack the cakes, spreading some buttercream between each layer.

3. Coat the cake in a thin layer of buttercream, to catch any excess cake crumbs. Chill the cake in the refrigerator for 20 minutes. Once chilled, coat the cake in a thick, generous layer of buttercream.

4. Place the remaining buttercream in a piping bag fitted with a large, star-shaped piping tip. Pipe little dollops onto the top of the cake. Sprinkle black sugar onto the dollops.

5. Gently press the black sprinkles onto the sides of the cake, placing a baking sheet under the cake to catch any that fall. Enjoy!

Glowing Ghosts Cake

MAKES A 9-INCH CAKE

Meringue ghosts glow atop a chocolate peanut butter cake with the help of hidden glow sticks! I recommend using short glow sticks, as they will be easier to conceal within the cake and ghosts. I chose to use purple glow sticks to match the ganache drizzle, but choose whichever color you like best!

Ghosts:
4 large egg whites, room temperature
½ teaspoon cream of tartar
1 cup superfine sugar
Edible ink pen
Glow sticks

Cake Batter:
1 cup unsalted butter, room temperature
2 cups sugar
1 teaspoon vanilla extract
6 eggs, room temperature
3 cups all-purpose flour
½ cup cocoa powder
1 teaspoon salt
1 teaspoon baking soda
1¼ cups buttermilk
1 cup chocolate chips

Buttercream:
½ cup peanut butter
1 cup unsalted butter, room temperature
1 teaspoon vanilla extract
2½ cups confectioners' sugar

Drizzle:
5 ounces white chocolate, melted
2½ ounces whipping cream, hot
Purple food coloring

Make the Ghosts:

1. Preheat the oven to 200°F and line a baking sheet with parchment paper.

2. Combine the egg whites and cream of tartar in a large bowl and beat with an electric mixer until foamy. Increase the speed of the mixer, and once the eggs become opaque, add ½ of the sugar. Continue beating until the egg whites start to stiffen. Add the remaining sugar and beat until stiff peaks form.

3. Place the mixture into a piping bag fitted with a large, round piping tip. Pipe dollops onto your prepared baking sheet, making several large ghosts and some smaller ghosts.

4. Bake for 60 to 90 minutes, until dry and crisp to the touch. Turn off the oven, open the oven door slightly, and leave the ghosts to dry completely, for 6 hours or up to overnight.

5. Gently draw faces onto the ghosts with the edible ink pen. Gently make small holes into the bottoms of the large ghosts with a sharp knife. Set aside.

Bake the Cake:

1. Preheat the oven to 350°F and grease and flour 2 (9-inch) round cake pans.

2. Beat butter and sugar with an electric mixer until fluffy. And vanilla and eggs, one at a time, mixing with each addition.

3. In a separate bowl, combine the flour, cocoa powder, salt, and baking soda. Add this to the batter in 2 additions, alternating with the buttermilk. Mix in the chocolate chips.

(Continued on next page)

4. Pour between your prepared pans and bake for 40 minutes, or until a skewer inserted into the cakes comes out clean. Cool completely.

Make the Buttercream:

1. Beat the peanut butter and butter with an electric mixer until smooth. Add the vanilla and combine. Add the confectioners' sugar 1 cup at a time, mixing with each addition.

Make the Drizzle:

1. Combine the melted white chocolate and hot whipping cream. Use a few drops of food coloring to dye the ganache purple and allow it to cool slightly while you assemble the cake.

Assembly:

1. Slice the tops off the cakes to level the surfaces. Spread some of the buttercream onto one cake and place the other on top. Spread some more buttercream on top of the cake and a scant amount on the sides.

2. Snap the glow sticks to trigger the glowing function, wrap in plastic wrap, and insert into the cake. Leave the top of the glow sticks sticking out of the cake.

3. Add the purple drizzle onto the cake, allowing it to drip off the sides. Slide the large ghosts onto the top of the glow sticks and decorate the rest of the cake with the small ghosts. Place the cake in a very dark room (or outside!) and watch the ghosts glow!

BLEEDING CAKE

MAKES A 9-INCH CAKE

This ultra spooky cake isn't just bloody on the outside! Slice into the cake to discover a tart raspberry pomegranate filling. I love this because not only does it make it even more fun to slice, but the tartness of the filling will cut through the sweetness of the cake and balance out the flavors perfectly.

Cake Batter:
1½ cups unsalted butter, room
   temperature
3 cups sugar
1½ teaspoons vanilla extract
9 large eggs, room temperature
4½ cups all-purpose flour
1 cup cocoa powder
1½ teaspoons baking soda
1½ teaspoons salt
1¾ cups sour cream

Buttercream:
4 cups unsalted butter, room
   temperature
2 teaspoons vanilla extract
10 cups confectioners' sugar

Filling:
1 cup raspberry jam
3 tablespoons pomegranate juice

Knives:
½ cup white candy melts, melted
Black food coloring
¼ cup dark chocolate chips, melted

Bloody Drip:
5 ounces white chocolate, melted
2 ounces heavy cream
Red food coloring

Bake the Cake:

1. Preheat the oven to 350°F and grease and flour 3 (9-inch) round cake pans.

2. Beat the butter and sugar with an electric mixer until pale and fluffy. Add the vanilla and eggs, one a time, mixing with each addition.

3. In a separate bowl, combine the flour, cocoa powder, baking soda, and salt. Add this to the batter in 2 additions, alternating with the sour cream.

4. Divide the batter between your prepared pans and bake for 40 minutes, or until a skewer inserted into the cakes come out clean. Cool in the pans for 10 minutes, then transfer to a wire rack and cool completely.

Make the Buttercream:

1. Beat the butter with an electric mixer until pale and fluffy. Add the vanilla and mix until combined. Add the confectioners' sugar 1 cup at a time, beating well with each addition.

Assembly:

1. Combine both filling ingredients in a bowl. Set aside.

2. Flatten the surfaces of the cakes with a serrated knife. Spread some buttercream onto the top of one cake, then place another cake on top. Carve a 4-inch circle out of the center of this layer, then remove. This will create a ring of cake with an open center cavity., Spread buttercream onto all walls of the center cavity. Place the cake in the refrigerator until the buttercream stiffens, about 20 minutes.

(Continued on page 35)

3. Pour the filling into the cavity, making sure to leave some space between the filling and the top of the cake. Spread some buttercream along the top of the cake, then place the remaining cake layer on top.

4. Coat the entire cake in an even layer of buttercream, then place in the refrigerator to chill for 20 minutes.

5. To make the knives, dye the white candy melts gray with 1 drop of black food coloring. Pour into a knife-shaped chocolate mold. Create the handles with melted dark chocolate. Place the mold in the freezer until the chocolate has set, about 15 minutes.

6. To make the bloody drip, combine the melted white chocolate and heavy cream. Add red food coloring and mix to combine.

7. Place the cake on your desired serving platter. Spoon the bloody drip onto the top edges of the cake, allowing it to drip off the sides. It may drip off the platter, so either have a sheet of parchment paper underneath to catch the dripping, or place it on your serving table and pour the blood onto the cake as guests arrive. They'll see the blood dripping onto the table! Then spread the blood drip over the top surface of the cake. Gently stick the chocolate knives into the cake. Enjoy!

Skull Cakes with Gooey Brains

MAKES 6 SMALL CAKES

These sweet skulls are dusted with confectioners' sugar and explode with strawberry brains when you slice into them!

Cake:
½ cup all-purpose flour
½ cup cornstarch
4 large eggs, whites and yolks separated
Pinch of salt
¾ cup sugar, separated
1 teaspoon vanilla extract

Filling:
½ cup whipping cream
½ teaspoon vanilla extract
2 tablespoons strawberry jam
Red food coloring
5 strawberries, finely chopped
Confectioners' sugar

Bake the Cake:

1. Preheat the oven to 350°F and grease and flour a skull-shaped cake mold.

2. Sift together the flour and cornstarch. Place the egg whites and salt in a bowl and beat with an electric mixer until soft peaks form. Gradually add ¼ cup sugar and mix until the egg whites are stiff and glossy. Set aside.

3. Place the egg yolks, vanilla, and ½ cup sugar in a large bowl and beat with an electric mixer until pale and thick. Fold the egg whites into the mixture. Add the flour mixture in 3 additions, folding to gently combine.

4. Pour the batter into your prepared skull pan and smooth the surface. Bake for 35 to 40 minutes, until a skewer inserted into the center comes out clean. Turn the cakes out onto a wire rack and let cool.

Make the Filling:

1. Combine the whipping cream and vanilla and beat with an electric mixer until stiff peaks form. Fold in the strawberry jam, a couple drops of food coloring, and fresh strawberries.

2. Cut off any edges of the cake that have spilled over during baking and flatten the bottom of each cake so that they sit nicely on your work surface. Carve a small hole out of the bottom of each cake, reserving the cake scraps. Spoon the strawberry cream into each hole, using some cake scraps to seal them closed.

3. Turn the cakes right side up, generously dust with confectioners' sugar, and enjoy!

Black Cat Cake

MAKES A 6-INCH CAKE

Would you let this cat cross your path? If you tasted how delicious and moist this chocolate cake recipe is, I have no doubt that you would! It's worth risking the bad luck for a slice of my favorite chocolate cake recipe.

Cake Batter:
2 cups all-purpose flour
2 cups sugar
¾ cup cocoa powder
2 teaspoons baking powder
1½ teaspoons baking soda
1 teaspoon salt
1 cup milk
½ cup vegetable oil
2 large eggs
2 teaspoons vanilla extract
1 cup boiling water

Buttercream:
2 cups unsalted butter, room temperature
2 tablespoons vanilla extract
½ cup milk
4 cups confectioners' sugar
1½ cups cocoa powder
1 tablespoon activated charcoal powder, or black food coloring (see page 29 for more information)

Decoration:
1 bubble tea straw, cut in half lengthwise
2 yellow candy melts
1 pink candy melt

Bake the Cake:

1. Preheat the oven to 350°F and grease and flour 2 (6-inch) round baking pans.

2. Combine the flour, sugar, cocoa powder, baking powder, baking soda, and salt in a large bowl.

3. Add the milk, vegetable oil, eggs, and vanilla and mix with an electric mixer until combined. Slowly add the boiling water and mix until well combined.

4. Divide the batter evenly between your prepared pans. Bake for 35 to 40 minutes, until a skewer inserted into the centers comes out clean. Cool for 15 minutes in the pan, then transfer to a wire rack and cool completely.

Make the Buttercream:

1. Beat the butter with an electric mixer until pale and fluffy. Add the vanilla and milk and mix well. Add the confectioners' sugar and cocoa powder 1 cup at a time, beating with each addition.

2. Dye the buttercream black with the charcoal powder and mix well.

Assembly:

1. Slice the tops and bottoms off the cakes to smooth the surface and remove any excess browning. Reserve the cake scraps for making the ears. Stack the cakes, spreading some buttercream between each layer.

(Continued on next page)

2. Coat the cake in a thin layer of buttercream to catch any excess crumbs. Crumble the cake scraps into a bowl and add about ½ cup of buttercream. Use the electric mixer to break apart the cake and mix it with the buttercream. This is essentially cake pop mix! Shape this mix into 2 ears and attach them to the cake with the help of a bubble tea straw to hold the structure. Coat the ears in a thin layer of buttercream. Chill the cake in the refrigerator for 20 minutes.

3. Place the remaining buttercream into a piping bag fitted with a large, grass-style piping tip. Pipe the buttercream all over the cake.

4. Press 2 yellow candy melts onto the cake as the eyes. Cut the pink candy melt into a triangle and stick onto the cake as the nose.

5. Place the remaining buttercream into a piping bag fitted with a small, round piping tip. Pipe pupils onto the yellow candy melts and enjoy your cat!

Pink Lemonade Halloween Cake

Love Halloween but not the classic colors? This cake is for you! This wonderfully fresh, tart lemon cake is actually my grandmother's recipe. She passed before I was born, so it gives me a warm, comforting feeling to bring her cake to life in my kitchen and share it with you! I've scattered fresh strawberries between the cake layers to cut through the sweetness of the cake and add a delicious, fruity vibrance. Tip: be sure to taste the lemon cake tops that you trim off while flattening the cakes. Thanks to the sugar lemon drizzle we pour on top, the cake tops are particularly divine and not something you want to miss out on tasting!

Cake Batter:

6 tablespoons + 2 cups sugar, divided
Juice from 2 lemons
1 cup unsalted butter, room temperature
4 large eggs
3 cups flour
2 teaspoons baking powder
1 teaspoons salt
1 cup milk
Zest of 4 lemons

Frosting:

2 cups unsalted butter, room temperature
5 cups confectioners' sugar
Zest from 3 lemons
2–3 teaspoons pure lemon extract
Juice from half a lemon
Pink food coloring
Black food coloring

Decoration:

8 fresh strawberries, diced
Eye and mustache sprinkles
Halloween candy

Bake the Cake:

1. Preheat the oven to 350°F and grease and flour 2 (6-inch) round cake pans.

2. Mix the 6 tablespoons sugar and lemon juice in a small bowl and set aside.

3. Place the butter in a large bowl and beat with an electric mixer until light and fluffy. Add 2 cups sugar and mix well. Add the eggs one at a time, beating well after each addition.

4. Sift together the flour, baking powder, and salt in a separate bowl. Add this to the butter mixture in 2 additions, alternating with milk. Add the lemon zest and fully combine.

5. Divide the batter evenly between your prepared pans and bake for 30 to 40 minutes, until a skewer inserted into the centers comes out clean.

6. Once the cakes come out of the oven, cool them in the pans for 10 minutes, then turn them out onto plates. Gently poke little holes into the top of the cakes with a toothpick, piercing the cake about ¾ of the way through. Spoon the lemon sugar mixture from step 2 onto the surface of each cake. The plates will catch any excess lemon sugar and allow it to soak back into the cakes.

(Continued on page 43)

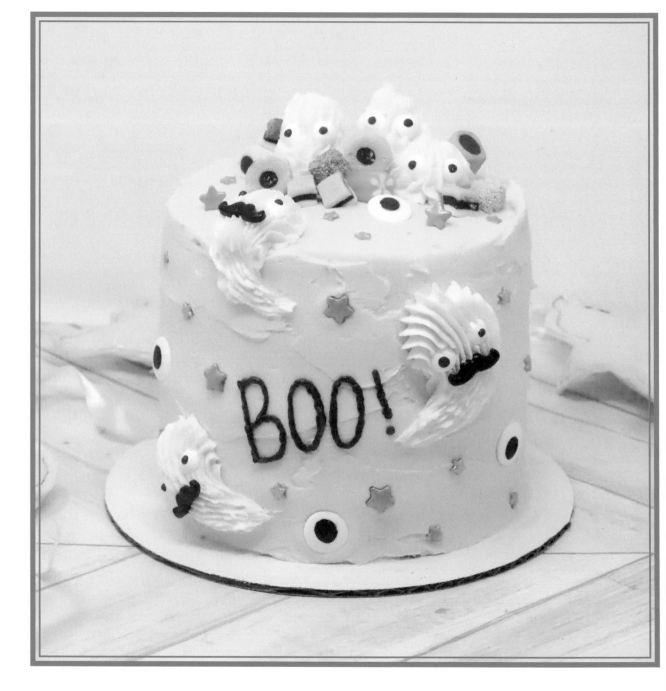

Make the Frosting:

1. Place the butter and sugar in a large bowl and beat with an electric mixer until light and fluffy. Add the lemon zest, lemon extract, and lemon juice and mix well. Set ½ cup of the frosting aside.

2. Dye the remaining large quantity of frosting pale pink with a bit of food coloring.

Assembly:

1. Slice the rounded tops off the cakes, then slice each cake horizontally into 2 layers. Stack the cakes and spread about ¼ cup of pink frosting between each layer. Scatter ⅓ of the strawberries on top of each layer of frosting. Coat the entire cake in a thin layer of pink frosting and place in the refrigerator to chill for 15 minutes.

2. Once chilled, coat the cake in a generous layer of pink frosting and use a cake spatula to smooth the surface.

3. Dye 2 tablespoons of the white frosting black with food coloring. Place it into a piping bag fitted with a small, round piping tip. Pipe "BOO!" onto the side of the cake with the black frosting.

4. Place the remaining white frosting into a piping bag fitted with a large, star-shaped piping tip. Pipe ghosts all over the cake. Stick candy eyes and mustaches onto the ghosts as you like.

5. Decorate the rest of the cake with other sprinkles and Halloween candy. Slice and enjoy!

Ouija Board Sheet Cake

MAKES A 9×11-INCH SHEET CAKE

As someone who has had some unexplainable supernatural experiences, I was honestly a little nervous making this cake. When I was taking the final photos, I was whispering under my breath that this cake was not an invitation for any spirits, no matter how hungry they were!

Cake Batter:

1 cup unsalted butter, room temperature
2 cups sugar
3 teaspoons vanilla extract
6 large eggs
3 cups all-purpose flour
1 teaspoon baking soda
1 teaspoon salt
1½ cups sour cream
1 tablespoon activated charcoal powder, or black food coloring (see page 29 for more information)
1 cup white chocolate chips

Decoration:

Plain Buttercream (page 3)
1 tablespoon activated charcoal powder, or black food coloring

Bake the Cake:

1. Preheat the oven to 350°F and grease and flour a 9×11 rectangular cake pan.

2. Beat the butter and sugar with an electric mixer until pale and smooth. Add the vanilla and eggs, one at a time, mixing with each addition.

3. In a separate bowl, combine the flour, baking soda, and salt. Add this to the batter in 2 additions, alternating with the sour cream. Divide the batter in half. Add the charcoal powder to half of the batter and mix until combined. Add the white chocolate chips to the remaining white batter. Fold to combine.

4. Carefully spoon large dollops of each color of batter into your prepared pan and bake for 35 to 45 minutes, or until a skewer inserted into the center comes out clean. Cool completely.

Assembly:

1. Reserve ¾ cup of buttercream and dye the remaining buttercream black with charcoal powder.

2. Place the cake on your work surface. Cover the entire cake evenly in the black buttercream and smooth the surface.

3. Use a toothpick or skewer to write all of the details, letters, and decorations of the Ouija board onto the cake. This will allow you to plan out your design before you start piping it on.

(Continued on next page)

4. Place the white buttercream into a piping bag with a medium-sized round piping tip. Pipe over the designs you made with the toothpick.

5. Use a butter knife or palette knife to spread some white buttercream onto the two bottom corners of the cake to make it look like a stormy cloud. Then put the remaining white buttercream into a piping bag fitted with a small, star-shaped piping tip. Pipe little stars and swirls on top of the clouds and in any other parts of the cake where you feel need an extra touch.

6. Then slice up the cake and hope that you don't have a ghostly guest at your dessert table!

Rose Gold Skull Cake

FILLS AN 8x4x5-INCH SKULL MOLD

I love this cake so much! I used a large 3D skull cake pan as a mold, which allowed me to create both the front and back of the skull. The cake sits upright on its own and is as exciting as a decoration as it is cake!

Vanilla Cake:

1 cup unsalted butter, room temperature
2 cups sugar
3 teaspoons vanilla extract
6 large eggs
3 cups all-purpose flour
1 teaspoon baking soda
1 teaspoon salt
1½ cups sour cream

Rose Buttercream:

2 cups unsalted butter, room temperature
1 teaspoon vanilla extract, or seeds from
  1 vanilla bean
1 tablespoon rose water
5 cups confectioners' sugar
2 cups pink candy melts
2 cups fresh raspberries
Rose gold edible food spray

Bake the Cake:

1. Preheat the oven to 350°F and grease and flour 3 (6-inch) round cake pans.

2. Beat the butter and sugar with an electric mixer until pale and smooth. Add the vanilla and eggs, one at a time, mixing with each addition.

3. In a separate bowl, combine the flour, baking soda, and salt. Add this to the batter in 2 additions, alternating with the sour cream.

4. Spoon the batter into your prepared pans and bake for 30 minutes, or until a skewer inserted into the centers comes out clean. Cool completely.

Make the Buttercream:

1. Beat the butter with an electric mixer until pale and fluffy. Add the vanilla, rose water, and confectioners' sugar 1 cup at a time, beating with each addition.

Assembly:

1. Place the candy melts in a microwave-safe bowl. Microwave for 30-second intervals until melted, stirring at each interval.

2. Coat the insides of a 3D skull cake pan with the candy melts. Place the cake pan in the refrigerator for 30 minutes until set.

3. Spread a second layer of candy melts into the pan and chill in the refrigerator for another 30 minutes.

(Continued on page 49)

4. Crumble the vanilla cakes into a fine crumb. Add 1 cup of buttercream at a time, mixing with each addition, until the cake crumbs retain their shape when pinched. Add the raspberries and fold until thoroughly combined.

5. Spoon the cake mixture into the hardened candy melt shell in the cake mold. Smooth the surface of the cake, so that both sides can come together and the candy melt shells can be sealed together in the next step.

6. Return the cake pan to the refrigerator to chill, about 30 minutes. Carefully unmold the cake-filled shells from the pan. Spread some extra melted candy melts along the edges of the shells and seal both sides together. Return the skull to the refrigerator until the seal has set.

7. Place the skull on your work surface and spray the surface evenly with rose gold edible food spray. Then serve by cracking open the skull and scooping out some cake!

CANDY CORN CAKE

What I love about candy corn is how quintessentially Halloween it is. What I do not like about candy corn is its taste. Luckily, we've found a workaround with this cake! Get all the cuteness of candy corn without the processed taste. This cake is a twist on my classic vanilla cake recipe, with the addition of pumpkin pie spice and maple syrup and substituting brown sugar for regular white sugar. It tastes fabulous!

Cake Batter:

1 cup unsalted butter, room temperature
2 cups brown sugar
3 teaspoons vanilla extract
¼ cup maple syrup
6 large eggs
3 cups all-purpose flour
1 teaspoon baking soda
1 teaspoon salt
2 teaspoons pumpkin pie spice
1½ cups sour cream
Orange and yellow food coloring

Decoration:

Plain Buttercream (page 3)
Orange and yellow food coloring

Bake the Cake:

1. Preheat oven to 350°F and grease and flour 3 (6-inch) round cake pans.

2. Beat the butter and brown sugar with an electric mixer until pale and smooth. Add the vanilla, maple syrup, and eggs one at a time, mixing with each addition.

3. In a separate bowl, combine the flour, baking soda, salt, and pumpkin pie spice. Add this to the batter in 2 additions, alternating with the sour cream. Divide the batter into 3 bowls. Leave one bowl white and dye the others each yellow and orange with a few drops of food coloring.

4. Spoon each different color of the batter into your prepared pans and bake for 30 minutes, or until a skewer inserted into the centers comes out clean. Cool completely.

Assembly:

1. Slice the tops and bottoms off the cakes to smooth the surface and remove any excess browning. Set aside the scraps from the white cake layer.

2. Stack the cakes, placing the yellow cake at the bottom, the orange in the middle, and the white cake on top. Spread ¼ cup of buttercream between each layer.

(Continued on next page)

3. Use a serrated knife to carve the cake into a candy corn shape, disregarding the top 2 or 3 inches where the point would be—we'll make that tip in the next step. Imagine a candy corn with a flat top—that's what you want to carve!

4. Crumble the remaining white cake scraps into fine crumbs. Add about 1 to 2 tablespoons of buttercream and mix well, until the cake crumbs retain their shape when rolled into a ball. You may need to add some extra buttercream (this is basically a cake pop mixture, and is a fabulous way to add shape to cakes without having to bake a whole extra layer). Place the mixture on top of the white layer and shape it into the top point of the candy corn.

5. Coat the cake in a thin layer of buttercream, called a crumb coat—this will catch any excess cake crumbs. Chill the cake in the refrigerator for 20 minutes.

6. Divide the remaining frosting into 3 bowls. Leave one bowl white and dye the remaining bowls orange and yellow with a bit of food coloring. Put all 3 colors in individual piping bags fitted with small, star-shaped piping tips.

7. Pipe the buttercream onto the cake in 3 large stripes, to look like a real candy corn!

HAUNTED HOUSE CAKE

MAKES A 6-INCH CAKE

I love the idea of making Halloween-themed gingerbread houses, but I can never bring myself to deal with wiggly cookie walls and the almost-certain mess that is royal icing. In my attempts to avoid such a fate, I've come up with this cake! It features my classic, moist chocolate cake as a base and has a rich chocolate cream cheese frosting. I experimented with the frosting recipe for this cookbook and I am in love with the result. It's so rich and pairs perfectly with the cake and the little nut cobblestone walls of the house.

Cake Batter:

2 cups all-purpose flour
2 cups sugar
¾ cup cocoa powder
2 teaspoons baking powder
1½ teaspoons baking soda
1 teaspoon salt
1 cup milk
½ cup vegetable oil
2 large eggs
2 teaspoon vanilla extract
1 cup boiling water

Buttercream:

9 ounces cream cheese, room
    temperature
1½ cups unsalted butter, room
    temperature
2 teaspoons vanilla extract
3 teaspoons ground cinnamon
    (optional)
3 cups confectioners' sugar
½ cup chocolate hazelnut spread
¼ cup cocoa powder
Red food coloring

Bake the Cake:

1. Preheat oven to 350°F and grease 4 (6-inch) round cake pans.

2. Combine the flour, sugar, cocoa powder, baking powder, baking soda, and salt in a large bowl.

3. Add the milk, vegetable oil, eggs, and vanilla and mix with an electric mixer until combined. Slowly add the boiling water and mix until well combined.

4. Divide the batter evenly between your prepared pans and bake for 30 to 35 minutes, until a skewer inserted into the center comes out clean. Cool for 15 minutes in the pan, then turn onto a wire rack and cool completely.

Make the Buttercream:

1. Place the cream cheese and butter in a bowl and beat with an electric mixer until smooth. Add the vanilla and cinnamon, if using, mix well. Add the confectioners' sugar 1 cup at a time, mixing with each addition.

2. Reserve ½ cup of buttercream and set aside for later. To the remaining large bowl of buttercream, add the chocolate hazelnut spread and cocoa powder. Mix well.

(Continued on page 55)

Decoration:

½ cup mixed nuts

½ cup chocolate-covered raisins

7 sticks of Pocky

1 cup Mini-Wheats

½ chocolate bar (something with fillings and nuts will give you a more rustic look)

¼ cup swirled chocolate chips

Black widow spider (page 13)

¼ cup black sprinkles

Assembly:

1. Slice the tops off 3 of the cakes. Cut the edges to shape them into squares (alternatively, you could use small square/rectangular pans to begin with). Don't throw out the scraps—you can use this for cake pops!

2. Cut the final cake into a roof shape, using the other cakes as a guide to shape it into a square.

3. Stack the cakes and spread some brown buttercream between each layer. Cover the cake in a thin layer of buttercream, then place the cake in the refrigerator for 20 to 30 minutes, until the buttercream has stiffened.

4. Cover the entire cake in a thick, generous layer of buttercream.

5. Stick some nuts and chocolate-covered raisins to the sides of the house as stones and use the Pocky sticks as a wooden door. Use Mini-Wheats as roof tiles and a chocolate bar as the chimney. Use a chocolate chip as the door handle by attaching it to the Pocky door with some buttercream. You can use extra chocolate chips as accents to fill empty space on the house. I also stuck a fondant black widow on the house for some spookiness.

6. Place the ½ cup of white buttercream into a piping bag fitted with a small, round piping tip. Pipe "KEEP OUT!" onto the front door.

7. Dye the remaining white buttercream red and place it in a piping bag fitted with a medium, round piping tip. Pipe dripping blood onto the roof, chimney, and sides of the house.

BLACKBERRY BAT CAKE

MAKES A 6-INCH CAKE

This cute little bat is purple on the outside and inside, thanks to fresh blackberries!

Cake Batter:
1 cup unsalted butter, room temperature
2 cups sugar
3 teaspoons vanilla extract
6 large eggs
3 cups all-purpose flour
1 teaspoon baking soda
1 teaspoon salt
1½ cups milk
Purple food coloring
2 cups fresh or frozen blackberries

Decoration:
2 cups purple candy melts
4 lollipop sticks
Silver star sprinkles
Plain Buttercream (page 3)
Purple food coloring
Black food coloring
6 tablespoons blackberry jam
Black edible glitter

Bake the Cake:

1. Preheat the oven to 350°F and grease and flour 3 (6-inch) round cake pans.

2. Beat the butter and sugar with an electric mixer until pale and smooth. Add the vanilla and eggs, one at a time, mixing with each addition.

3. In a separate bowl, combine the flour, baking soda, and salt. Add this to the batter in 2 additions, alternating with the milk. Add 3 to 4 drops of purple food coloring to dye the cake batter purple. Add the blackberries and gently fold the batter with a spatula to combine.

4. Divide the batter between your prepared pans and bake for 35 to 45 minutes, or until a skewer inserted into the centers comes out clean. Cool completely.

Make the Ears and Wings:

1. Place the purple candy melts in a microwave-safe bowl and microwave for 30-second intervals until melted, stirring at each interval.

2. Set out a flat tray and line it with parchment paper. Gently spoon the candy melts onto the parchment paper into the shape of 2 ears and 2 wings. If desired, you can draw the shapes on a piece of paper, and place it under the parchment paper to use as a guide.

3. Before the candy melts set, poke lollipop sticks into the ears and wings, so that they will be able to be inserted into the cake. Sprinkle some silver star sprinkles onto the wings and ears.

(Continued on next page)

4. Leave the ears and wings to set at room temperature, or in the refrigerator if you are in a hurry.

1. Set ¼ cup of buttercream aside and dye it black. Set 2 tablespoons of buttercream aside and keep it white. Dye the remaining large quantity of buttercream purple with food coloring.

2. Slice the tops and bottoms off the cakes to smooth the surface and remove any excess browning. Stack the cakes and spread some purple buttercream and 3 tablespoons of blackberry jam between each layer.

3. Coat the cake in a thin layer of purple buttercream to catch any excess crumbs. Chill the cake in the refrigerator for 20 minutes. Once chilled, coat the cake in a smooth, thick layer of purple buttercream.

4. Stick the wings into the sides of the cake and the ears into the top of the cake. Place the remaining purple buttercream into a piping bag fitted with a small, star-shaped piping tip. Pipe dollops around the ears to look like fur. Sprinkle some black edible glitter onto the fur.

5. Place the black buttercream into a piping bag fitted with a round, medium-sized piping tip. Pipe the bat's eyes and mouth onto the cake. Place the white buttercream into a piping bag fitted with a medium-small round piping tip. Pipe the fangs just underneath the mouth. Then slice and enjoy!

CANDY APPLE CAKE

MAKES 1 BUNDT CAKE

This delicious brown sugar Bundt cake looks like a ring of candy apples, which is arguably easier to eat than real candy apples! Decorate the apples with your favorite candy and surprise your friends with this adorable treat.

Cake Batter:
1 cup unsalted butter, room temperature
2 cups brown sugar
3 teaspoons vanilla extract
6 large eggs
3 cups all-purpose flour
1 teaspoon baking soda
1 teaspoon salt
2 tablespoons ground cinnamon
1½ cups sour cream

Buttercream:
2 cups unsalted butter, room temperature
1 teaspoon vanilla extract
3 drops graham cracker flavor (optional;
    I bought Wilton's brand)
4½ cups confectioners' sugar
Green, brown, and orange food coloring
¼ cup dulce de leche
¼ cup each of assorted candy, chopped into
    pieces if necessary
6 candy apple skewers

Bake the Cake:
1. Preheat oven to 350°F and grease and flour a Bundt pan.

2. Beat the butter and brown sugar with an electric mixer until pale and smooth. Add the vanilla and eggs, one at a time, mixing with each addition.

3. In a separate bowl, combine the flour, baking soda, salt, and cinnamon. Add this to the batter in 2 additions, alternating with the sour cream.

4. Pour the batter into your prepared pan and bake for 45 to 60 minutes or until a skewer inserted into the cake comes out clean. Cool completely.

Make the Buttercream:
1. Beat the butter with an electric mixer until pale and fluffy. Add the vanilla and graham cracker flavor, if using, and mix well. Add the confectioners' sugar 1 cup at a time, beating with each addition.

Assembly:
1. Use a serrated knife to carve the Bundt cake into 6 connected spheres. Cut little craters into the top of each sphere to create the dip where the apples' stems would be.

2. Carefully coat the entire cake in a thin layer of buttercream. Place the cake in the refrigerator and chill for 20 minutes.

(Continued on page 61)

3. Divide the remaining buttercream in half. Dye one half green with a few drops of food coloring. Set the other half aside.

4. Spread the green buttercream onto the top halves of the apples. Be sure to smooth the buttercream as best as you can and coat the inside of the craters as well.

5. Add the dulce de leche to the remaining white buttercream. If you would like the buttercream to be darker, add a couple drops of brown and 1 drop of orange food coloring to make it look like caramel!

6. Spread the caramel buttercream onto the bottom halves of the apples. Spread the buttercream up to meet the green buttercream to make sure no cake is showing.

7. Place the cake in the refrigerator for 20 to 30 minutes, for the buttercream to stiffen.

8. Working with one "apple" at a time, spread another layer of caramel buttercream onto the caramel portion. Because the cake has been chilled, you'll be able to apply the caramel buttercream on top of the green buttercream, if necessary, without the green buttercream smudging. This will create a more natural look and allow you to spread the caramel frosting as high onto the apples as you'd like.

9. Once the second layer of caramel buttercream has been spread onto an apple, stick on the candy toppings. The second, fluffy layer of buttercream will allow the candies to stick firmly, while the cool base of the cake will encourage the buttercream to slightly stiffen and further secure the candies. This way, you won't have candies falling off the apples!

10. Repeat with the remaining apples, covering them generously with buttercream and candy.

11. Stick the candy apple skewers into each apple and serve!

Pumpkin Bundt Cake

MAKES 1 BUNDT CAKE

This cute, festive Bundt cake has a cheesecake layer ribboned throughout that melts during baking, giving the already decadent and moist pumpkin cake an incredible depth of autumn flavor. My favorite cream cheese frosting is swirled on top and the stem is a fun take on classic crispy rice treats, but uses granola instead!

Pumpkin Batter:
Cooking spray
4 large eggs
3 cups sugar
3 cups canned plain pumpkin puree
1 cup unsalted butter, melted
5 cups all-purpose flour, plus more for
    dusting
4 teaspoons baking soda
1 teaspoon salt
2 teaspoons pumpkin spice mix

Cheesecake Layer:
1 large egg
½ cup sugar
8 ounces cream cheese, room
    temperature
1 tablespoon all-purpose flour
1 teaspoon pumpkin pie spice

Frosting:
1½ cups unsalted butter, room
    temperature
9 ounces cream cheese, room
    temperature
1 teaspoon vanilla extract
3 cups confectioners' sugar
Orange food coloring

Bake the Cake:

1. Preheat the oven to 350°F. Coat a Bundt pan with cooking spray, and dust it with flour.

2. Make the pumpkin batter by whisking together the eggs, sugar, pumpkin puree, and butter in a large bowl.

3. In a separate bowl, mix the flour, baking soda, salt, and pumpkin spice mix, and add to the pumpkin mixture and mix. Set aside.

4. Prepare the cheesecake layer by mixing the egg, sugar, and cream cheese in a bowl. Beat with an electric mixer until smooth. Add the flour and pumpkin pie spice and mix until combined. Set aside.

5. Spoon ⅓ of the pumpkin batter into the pan and smooth the surface. Drizzle half of the cheesecake layer on top. Repeat with another ⅓ of the pumpkin batter, then the remaining cheesecake layer, then the final ⅓ of the pumpkin batter.

6. Smooth the surface and place the pan on a baking sheet to catch any cake batter that may spill over.

7. Bake for 50 to 60 minutes, or until a skewer inserted into the cake comes out clean. If the surface of the cake is browning too quickly, loosely cover the top of the cake with aluminum foil.

8. Once the cake is fully cooked, allow it to cool completely in the pan.

(Continued on next page)

Stem:

2 tablespoons unsalted butter
2½ cups mini marshmallows
¼ teaspoon vanilla extract
3 cups granola
½ cup dark green fondant

Make the Frosting:

1. Beat the butter and cream cheese with an electric mixer until fluffy. Add the vanilla and combine. Add the confectioners' sugar and beat until light and fluffy.

2. Dye the frosting orange with food coloring.

Make the Stem:

1. Melt the butter in a pot over low heat. Add the mini marshmallows and mix until fully melted. Remove from the heat and add the vanilla. Add the granola and mix well.

2. Allow the mixture to cool until it is easily handled. Spray your hands with cooking spray and shape it into the pumpkin's stem. Set aside.

Assembly:

1. Unmold the Bundt cake and place it on your work surface. Cover the entire cake in a generous layer of frosting. Make pretty swirls in the frosting for an even more glamorous look.

2. Stick the granola stem into the center of the cake.

3. Shape the fondant into a pumpkin leaf, using a maple leaf cookie cutter. They look very similar to pumpkin leaves! Roll the remaining fondant into long, thin ropes, then form them into curls, to create the pumpkin vines. Stick these onto the cake and enjoy!

WORM CHEESECAKE

MAKES A 9-INCH CHEESECAKE

I hesitate to admit this, but this was one of my recipes that even I was too grossed out to eat! Even having made it with my own hands, I couldn't bring myself to put one of those wiggly worms anywhere near my plate. It might also have to do with the fact that I served this to my family for dessert on Canadian Thanksgiving, as I had made it fresh the day before. Quite a unique dessert for Thanksgiving, but definitely a memorable one!

Worms:
2 boxes raspberry Jell-O
3 packets powdered gelatin
3 cups boiling water
¾ cup whipping cream
15 drops green food coloring
100 flexible straws
Mason jar

Cheesecake Base:
7 ounces chocolate wafers
4 tablespoons unsalted butter, melted

Cheesecake Filling:
16 ounces cream cheese, room temperature
1 tablespoon cocoa powder
½ cup granulated sugar
1¾ cups whipping cream
¼ cup lemon juice (from about 1 lemon)
½ teaspoon vanilla extract
2 teaspoons powdered gelatin
2½ tablespoons cold water
Oreo cookie crumbs

Make the Worms:

1. Combine the Jell-O powder and powdered gelatin in a large bowl. Add the boiling water and stir until dissolved. Place the bowl in the refrigerator for 20 minutes, or until lukewarm.

2. In a separate bowl, combine the whipping cream and green food coloring (this will help tone down the pink color and make the worms more realistic). Add to the Jell-O mixture and mix well.

3. Extend the flexible straws and insert them into a tall mason jar, flexible ends downward. The straws should fit snugly into the jar. Wrap an elastic band around the straws, then slowly pour the mixture into the straws. It will pour out into the mason jar as well, but don't worry! Keep pouring until the mason jar is full. Place the jar into the refrigerator and leave overnight.

4. Gently pull the straws out of the mason jar (this may take a little wiggling). Working with one straw at a time, run it under hot water, then squeeze one end and push the worm out onto a plate. Repeat with the remaining straws, then place in the refrigerator while you make the cheesecake.

Make the Base:

1. Place the chocolate wafers in a food processor and pulse until they resemble a fine crumb. Add the butter and mix well. Press into the bottom of a 9-inch springform pan, then place the pan in the refrigerator while you make the filling.

(Continued on page 67)

Make the Filling:

1. Place the cream cheese in a bowl and beat with an electric mixer until smooth. Add the cocoa powder and sugar and combine. Then add the whipping cream, lemon juice, and vanilla, and mix until smooth.

2. Combine the gelatin and water in a small bowl and microwave for 30 seconds. Add the gelatin to the filling, and mix with an electric mixer until fully combined.

3. Scatter a few worms into the cheesecake pan, directly on top of the crust. Spoon some filling on top, then add a few more worms. Pour the rest of the filling on top and smooth the surface. Scatter ⅓ of the remaining worms on top, then place the cheesecake in the refrigerator until set, about 3 hours.

4. Slide a sharp knife around the edges of the cheesecake, then remove the sides of the pan.

5. Toss the remaining worms with some cookie crumbs, until they appear to be covered in dirt. Sprinkle some more crumbs onto the surface of the cheesecake, then scatter the worms on top. Enjoy!

Zombie Unicorn Cake

MAKES A 6-INCH CAKE

The spookiest unicorn you'll ever come across! This unicorn has green skin and a dark, spooky rainbow of layers inside. Be sure to duck away from its bloody horn and exposed brain—this zombie unicorn is hungry and might eat you first!

Cake Batter:

1 cup unsalted butter, room temperature
2 cups sugar
3 teaspoons vanilla extract
6 large eggs
3 cups all-purpose flour
1 teaspoon baking soda
1 teaspoon salt
1½ cups sour cream
Pink, orange, yellow, green, blue, purple, and black food coloring

Buttercream:

3 cups unsalted butter, room temperature
1½ teaspoons vanilla extract
7 cups confectioners' sugar
Brown, green, black, pink, yellow, and blue food coloring
½ cup white fondant
1 large marshmallow
Black sanding sugar
Red food coloring
¼ cup strawberry jam

Bake the Cake:

1. Preheat oven to 350°F and grease and flour 6 (6-inch) round cake pans.

2. Beat butter and sugar with an electric mixer until pale and smooth. Add vanilla and eggs, one at a time, mixing with each addition.

3. In a separate bowl, combine the flour, baking soda, and salt. Add this to the batter in 2 additions, alternating with the sour cream. Divide the batter into 6 bowls, and dye one each pink, orange, yellow, green, blue, and purple. Add 1 to 2 drops of black food coloring to each bowl, to give a gray tint to each color.

4. Spoon each colored bowl of batter between your prepared cake pans. Bake for 20 to 30 minutes, or until a skewer inserted into the centers comes out clean. Cool completely.

Make the Buttercream:

1. Beat the butter with an electric mixer until pale and fluffy. Add vanilla and mix until combined. Add the confectioners' sugar 1 cup at a time, mixing with each addition. Then beat for 3 to 5 minutes, until fluffy.

2. Dye all of the buttercream pale muddy green, by adding a small drop of brown along with the green. This will be for the cake layers and skin color of the unicorn, as well as the base for the other colors we use.

Assembly:

1. To make the horn, roll the white fondant into 2 (5-inch long) ropes. Wrap both around a chopstick or skewer, creating a spiral pattern that is thinner and more pointed toward the top, and using the stick to create extra support. Make sure about 3 to 4 inches of stick is exposed from the bottom of the horn—this will be used to secure it into the cake. Place the horn on a plate lined with plastic wrap and set aside to stiffen while you decorate the cake.

(Continued on next page)

2. Slice the tops and bottoms off the cakes to remove any excess browning. Stack them in the order of the rainbow, spreading some muddy green buttercream between each layer. Coat the entire cake in a thin layer of buttercream, then place in the refrigerator to chill for 20 minutes.

3. Mark where you will be placing the horn, then carve out a small cavity next to this (where the brain will be exposed). Make this spot slightly deeper than you think you'll need. Then cover the entire cake, including the cavity, in a thicker layer of buttercream.

4. Divide the remaining green buttercream into 4 bowls. Dye one each black, pink, yellow, and blue. Don't worry if the green base makes the colors look muddy—we want it to look like this!

5. Place each color of buttercream into separate piping bags and snip off the tips to create a medium-sized hole. For the black buttercream, just create a small hole at the tip of the piping bag.

6. Pipe a brain with the pink buttercream into the head cavity. It doesn't have to be perfect, just needs to look wiggly! Pipe the unicorn's eyes with the black buttercream.

7. Place a large, star-shaped piping tip (#2D) at the base of another piping bag. Pipe the pink, yellow, and blue buttercream into the bag in vertical stripes, alternating with a thin stripe of black buttercream. Use this multi-colored frosting to pipe the mane onto the unicorn. Don't make it too clean—a little disheveled will look good!

8. Slice the large marshmallow in half diagonally. Dunk the sticky side of the marshmallows into the black sanding sugar. Stick the ears onto the cake.

9. Stick the horn onto the cake. Dab a paper towel lightly into some red food coloring and then onto the tip of the unicorn horn, to look like blood. If desired, dab some more food coloring onto the sides of the cake to look like wounds.

10. Spoon some strawberry jam onto the brain, allowing it to drip down the sides of the cake. Enjoy!

CARAMEL APPLE CAKE POPS

MAKES ABOUT 20 CAKE POPS

Caramel apples are so wonderfully festive this time of the year, but not everyone wants to tackle an entire apple. These cute cake pops are made with my favorite spiced apple cake and decorated to look like cute little caramel apples. The perfect choice for when you're feeling festive, but only want a couple bites at a time.

1¾ cups all-purpose flour
2⅓ teaspoons baking powder
½ teaspoon salt
2 teaspoons ground cinnamon
½ teaspoon ground allspice
½ teaspoon ground nutmeg
¼ teaspoon ground cloves
½ cup unsalted butter, cold and cut into small cubes
½ cup light brown sugar
1 large egg
6–8 tablespoons milk
½ Granny Smith apple, grated
1½ cups vanilla frosting
¼ cup dulce de leche
Red, green, white, and yellow candy melts
3 teaspoons vegetable shortening, divided
Lollipop sticks
1 cup butterscotch chips

Make the Cake Pops:

1. Preheat oven to 350°F and grease a loaf pan well.

2. Combine the flour, baking powder, salt, cinnamon, allspice, nutmeg, and cloves in a large bowl.

3. Cut in the butter using a pastry blender or 2 knives. Add the brown sugar and egg and mix well.

4. Gradually add the milk until you have a smooth, thick batter. Add the grated apple and mix well. Pour into your prepared pan. Smooth the surface and bake for 40 minutes, or until a skewer inserted into the middle comes out clean.

5. Cool the cake in the pan for 15 minutes, then turn out onto a wire rack to cool completely.

6. Slice off the outside edges of the cake and crumble into a fine crumb. Combine the vanilla frosting and dulce de leche in a bowl, then add to the crumbs and mix until fully combined. The mixture should be able to maintain its shape. Roll the cake into balls and place on a tray lined with plastic wrap. Transfer to the freezer until firm, about 20 minutes.

7. Place some red and green candy melts into two microwave-safe bowls. If desired, add some white and yellow candy melts to the green candy melts to create a more vibrant color. Microwave for 30-second intervals until fully melted. Add 1 teaspoon vegetable shortening to each bowl and mixed until fully melted.

(Continued on page 73)

8. Reshape the cake balls so they're even. Stick a lollipop stick slightly into red or green candy melts, then gently insert into the top of a cake pop (this will help it stay stabilized). Repeat with the remaining cake pops and lollipop sticks, using either the red or green candy melts. Return the cake pops to the freezer until firm, about 10 minutes.

9. Dunk the cake pops into red or green candy melts, fully covering them. Return them to the baking sheet and place in the freezer until the candy melts have hardened, about 15 minutes.

10. Place the butterscotch chips into a microwave-safe bowl and microwave for 10 second intervals until melted. Add the remaining teaspoon of vegetable shortening and mix until fully melted and combined.

11. Dunk each cake pop halfway into the butterscotch chips. Return to the freezer until the candy melts have set, then enjoy!

Pumpkin Cake Pops

MAKES 12-20 CAKE POPS, DEPENDING ON SIZE

These sweet little pumpkins can be considered cake pops or truffles, since technically they're not on a lollipop stick. Whatever you may call them, they are divine. Cake pops are typically made with cake crumbs and buttercream, but in this recipe we're swapping the buttercream with white chocolate ganache. This gives the cake pops a rich, smooth texture and slightly elevated flavor.

13 ounces of Chocolate Pumpkin Cupcakes
    (page 11)
4 ounces white chocolate chips
2½ ounces whipping cream, hot
2 cups orange candy melts
Shortening or Wilton EZ Thin, as needed
Green fondant, or green gummies

1. Crumble up the cake until it is a fine crumb.

2. In a microwave-safe bowl, melt the chocolate chips for 30-second intervals until melted. Add the hot cream and mix until fully combined. Add this mixture to the crumbled cake and mix very well until combined.

3. Place the mixture in the freezer for 20 minutes, to stiffen.

4. Shape the mixture into 12 to 20 balls, making an indent in the center. Place on a plate, then freeze for 30 to 40 minutes, or until stiff.

5. Melt the orange candy melts in a melting pot or in a microwave-safe bowl for 30 second intervals, until fully melted. If you find the candy melts are too thick, add a little bit of shortening, as needed.

6. Dunk the cake pops into the melts one at a time, fully coating them. Use a fork to remove them from the pot, tapping them on the side to remove any excess. Place on a baking sheet lined with parchment paper.

7. While the candy melts are still wet, stick a stem and a curly accent made from fondant onto the pumpkin. It's best to do this right after dunking each cake pop into the candy melts.

8. Place the cake pops in the refrigerator to chill for 5 minutes, or until the candy melts have stiffened and enjoy!

Other Baked Goods & Sweet Treats

Skeleton Macarons

MAKES ABOUT 12

These delicious vanilla macarons are filled with my favorite classic chocolate hazelnut spread, which is always a good thing! The skeleton faces are drawn on with an edible ink pen. I love this technique because it's so much easier than piping royal icing or buttercream. Be sure to press gently, as the macarons are quite delicate.

1 cup confectioners' sugar
¾ cup almond flour (not almond meal)
2 large egg whites
Pinch of cream of tartar
¼ cup superfine sugar
1 teaspoon vanilla extract
Black edible ink pen
½ cup chocolate hazelnut spread, for filling

1. Combine the confectioners' sugar and almond flour in a bowl, then sift all together 3 times.

2. Place the egg whites in a large bowl and beat with an electric mixer until foamy. Add the cream of tartar, then beat until soft peaks form. Add the superfine sugar and beat on high speed until stiff peaks form. Add the vanilla and gently mix to combine. Sift the dry mixture into the egg mixture and gently fold to combine.

3. Place the mixture into a piping bag fitted with a large, round piping tip.

4. Pipe rounds onto a baking sheet lined with parchment paper or a Silpat baking sheet.

5. Tap the baking sheets on your countertop a couple times to remove any air bubbles. Let the macarons sit at room temperature for 30 minutes.

6. Set your oven to 375°F, heat for 5 minutes, then reduce the heat to 325°F. Put one pan in the oven right away once you reduce the heat. Bake the macarons, one sheet at a time, for 6 to 8 minutes, rotating halfway through. After each batch, increase the heat to 375°F, heat for 5 minutes, then reduce to 325°F and pop the next sheet into the oven!

7. Cool the macarons completely on the cookie sheet.

8. Draw the skeleton's face onto half of the macarons with the edible ink pen.

9. Place some chocolate hazelnut spread in a piping bag fitted with a round piping tip. Pipe onto the undecorated macarons and place a decorated macaron on top. Enjoy!

Mini Pumpkin Pie Gravestones

MAKES 9 HAND PIES

These are the most delicious hand pies you'll ever try! The pie dough recipe is a classic, and the filling is absolutely delicious. Pumpkin and white chocolate are a fabulous duo and are taken even further with cream cheese and crushed graham crackers. This filling also works great for peanut-butter-cup-style treats or as cream puff filling!

Pie Dough:

2½ cups all-purpose flour

1 teaspoon pumpkin pie spice

1 teaspoon salt

1 teaspoon sugar

1 cup cold unsalted butter, cut into cubes

¼–½ cup cold water

1 egg, beaten

Filling:

⅓ cup roughly crushed graham crackers

¼ cup plain canned pumpkin

½ cup white chocolate chips, melted

1–2 teaspoons pumpkin pie spice

1 ounce cream cheese, room temperature

1 tablespoon confectioners' sugar

Decoration:

3 tablespoons whipping cream

½ teaspoon vanilla extract

½ cup confectioners' sugar

Pinch of cinnamon

1 cup buttercream (page 3)

Black food coloring

Make the Dough:

1. Mix the flour, pumpkin pie spice, salt, and sugar in a food processor. Add butter and pulse until it turns into a crumbly texture. Drizzle ¼ cup cold water over, and pulse until the dough sticks together when pinched, adding a bit more water as needed. Shape the dough into a ball and wrap in plastic wrap. Place in the refrigerator for 1 hour, until firm.

Make the Filling:

1. Place all ingredients in a blender and pulse until smooth. Transfer to a piping bag and chill in the freezer for 15 minutes, or until stiffened slightly. This will make it easier to pipe!

Assembly:

1. Preheat oven to 400°F. Roll out the pie dough onto a floured surface, to an 18×14-inch rectangle. Trim the edges with a sharp knife. Slice into 9 rectangles.

2. Pipe the filling onto half of each rectangle. Fold the rectangles in half, then seal all four sides with a fork. Trim the edges on one end to create gravestone shapes. Brush the surface with the beaten egg.

3. Bake for 20 minutes, until golden. Then transfer to a wire rack and cool completely.

4. To make the glaze, combine the whipping cream, vanilla, confectioners' sugar, and cinnamon in a bowl. Spoon on top of the pop tarts and allow it to set, about 1 hour.

5. Dye the buttercream gray with just a bit of black food coloring. Place it into a piping bag fitted with a small, round piping tip. Pipe gravestone details and names onto the pop tarts with the buttercream.

6. Serve and enjoy!

Voodoo Doll Brownies

MAKES ABOUT 12

These are my favorite fudgy brownies and I'm so excited to share them with you! Kick them up a notch by adding 1 tablespoon instant coffee powder to the brownie batter. You won't taste the coffee flavor, it will just make the brownies even richer!

12 ounces bittersweet chocolate
1 cup unsalted butter
3 cups sugar
6 eggs
½ cup cocoa powder
Pinch of salt
1¼ cups all-purpose flour
1 cup vanilla buttercream (page 3)
Candy hearts

1. Preheat the oven to 350°F. Butter a 10×15-inch Swiss roll pan and line it with parchment paper, ensuring that excess parchment paper is hanging off of both sides.

2. Place the bittersweet chocolate and butter in a heatproof bowl over a pot of simmering water. Stir until fully melted, then remove from the heat.

3. Gradually whisk in the sugar and add the eggs one at a time, mixing after each addition. Add the cocoa powder and the pinch of salt.

4. Gently fold the flour into the mixture with a rubber spatula.

5. Pour the mixture into your prepared pan. Smooth the surface of the batter and bake for 35 to 50 minutes or until fully cooked.

6. Place the pan on a wire rack and allow the brownies to cool completely while still in the pan.

7. Use the overhanging parchment paper to lift the brownies from the pan. Use a gingerbread man cookie cutter to cut out doll shapes.

8. Place the buttercream into a piping bag fitted with a small, round piping tip. Pipe faces and stitches onto the dolls, and add candy heart accents where desired. Enjoy!

BRAINY BAKED ALASKA

SERVES 4-6

Baked Alaska is a fun dessert where ice cream is covered in toasted meringue. To toast the meringue, you'll need a handheld kitchen torch, which can be a little intimidating to use at first. Just make sure you're working in a well-ventilated area and brûlée away!

Filling:
3 cups cherry ice cream, slightly
   softened
7–8 chocolate sandwich cookies,
   crushed into large pieces

Topping:
6 egg whites
Pinch of cream of tartar
1 cup sugar
Pink food coloring

Make the Filling:
1. Line a 7.5×6-inch brain mold with plastic wrap, leaving enough plastic wrap for the excess to hang out over the sides.

2. Spoon the ice cream into the mold, sprinkling the crushed cookies into the ice cream as you spoon it in.

3. Fold the excess plastic wrap over the top of the ice cream and place the mold in the freezer overnight, or until frozen solid.

Make the Meringue Topping:
1. Place the egg whites and cream of tartar in a bowl and whip on high speed with an electric mixer for 2 minutes. Gradually add the sugar while whipping until stiff peaks form.

2. Add 1 to 2 drops of pink food coloring and gently mix to combine.

Assembly:
1. Remove the plastic wrap from the surface, then turn the brain out onto a plate lined with parchment paper. If you're having trouble removing it from the pan, warm the pan with a hot cloth. Remove the remaining plastic wrap from the brain and spread an even layer of meringue over the entire surface.

2. Place the remaining meringue in a piping bag filled with a large, round piping tip and pipe a brain pattern all over the brain.

3. Using a kitchen blowtorch, brown the edges of the meringue. Serve immediately and store the leftovers in the freezer.

Salted Caramel Skull Truffles

MAKES ABOUT 6 (1½-INCH) TRUFFLES

I never miss an opportunity to share my homemade dulce de leche recipe because it's just such a fun, unorthodox method! I was blown away when I tried this method the first time and have loved using it as a filling in white chocolate truffles. For an extra gourmet touch, stick some salted peanuts into the filling. They taste amazing with white chocolate and caramel.

1 can condensed milk
Large pinch of salt
2 cups white candy melts or white
    chocolate
Bronze edible luster dust

1. Place the unopened can of condensed milk in a pot and add enough water to fully submerge the can.

2. Set the pot to high heat and boil for 3 hours, or simmer for 6 hours. Drain the hot water and rinse the can in cold water for a few minutes, so it isn't too hot to handle. Open the can of condensed milk to discover homemade dulce de leche!

3. Pour the dulce de leche into a bowl and add a large pinch of salt, to taste. Mix and set aside.

4. Place some white candy melts into a microwave-safe bowl and microwave for 30-second intervals until melted, stirring at each interval.

5. Coat the insides of a skull-shaped mold with the melted candy or white chocolate. Place the mold in the refrigerator until the candy melts have set.

6. Spoon some dulce de leche into the truffle shells, then seal the shells closed with more candy melts. Return the mold to the refrigerator for about 30 minutes, until fully set.

7. Unmold the truffles and place them on your work surface. Use a clean brush to add some of the bronze edible dust and dust it over the features of the skull, including the teeth, nose, eyes, cheeks, and forehead. Enjoy!

Black Charcoal Ice Cream Cones

MAKES ABOUT 10-15 CONES

Homemade ice cream cones have always seemed like a fun, yet completely unnecessary kitchen adventure. But to be entirely honest, the most difficult part was getting around to buying the waffle cone maker! The process is quite similar to making pancakes and offers so many customization options, such as melted chocolate or marshmallows hidden in the base of the cones, or swirly, multicolored cone designs.

2 large eggs
½ cup white sugar
¼ cup unsalted butter, melted and cooled
3 tablespoons milk
½ teaspoon vanilla extract
⅓ cup all-purpose flour
½ tablespoon edible activated charcoal (see page 29 for more information)
Pinch of salt

1. Beat the eggs and sugar with an electric mixer until frothy. Add the butter, milk, and vanilla and mix until combined. In a separate bowl, combine the flour, charcoal, and salt. Add to the batter and mix until combined.

2. Spoon about 2 tablespoons of batter onto a waffle cone maker and cook for 1 minute. Roll it into a cone and keep on the cone-shaping tool until cool and stiffened, about 1 minute. Repeat with the remaining batter.

3. Enjoy!

Black Charcoal Ice Cream

MAKES 7-8 CUPS

Although this is technically not a baked good, I had to pair the ice cream with the cones! This is my classic ice cream recipe and I'm so excited to add some spookiness with a touch of charcoal. This may temporarily make your tongue and teeth black, so don't eat it on the way to a fancy party, unless it's a Halloween theme!

1½ cups whipping cream

2 tablespoons edible activated charcoal (see page 29 for more information)

4 eggs

¾ cup sugar

1 teaspoon vanilla extract

1. Beat the whipping cream and activated charcoal with an electric mixer until it forms a thick ribbon when the whisk is lifted.

2. In a separate bowl, whisk the eggs and add the sugar and vanilla. Beat well with an electric mixer until the mixture forms a ribbon when the whisk is lifted and the ribbon remains on the surface of the mixture for a few seconds.

3. Add half the egg mixture to the whipped cream and whisk together. Add the remaining egg mixture and gently fold the mixture to combine. Make sure to be gentle and keep the mixture as airy as possible.

4. Pour the ice cream into a Tupperware container, and seal with the lid. Place this in the freezer for 7 to 8 hours to chill and set.

HALLOWEEN CANDY SHORTBREAD COOKIES

MAKES ABOUT 24 (2-INCH) COOKIES

Shortbread cookies are one of my favorite cookies to make because of that delicate kiss of salt you get with each bite. I thought it would be fun to combine these cookies with something most of us have an excess of this time of year—leftover Halloween candy! I recommend staying away from hard candies and gummies, as they could melt during baking and ruin the texture of the cookies. Chocolate-based goodies are definitely the safer option!

1 cup unsalted butter, room temperature
½ cup confectioners' sugar
1 teaspoon vanilla extract
2 cups all-purpose flour
¾ teaspoon salt
1 cup extra Halloween candy, finely
  chopped

1. Preheat oven to 325°F and line a baking sheet with parchment paper.

2. Beat the butter with an electric mixer until pale and fluffy. Add the confectioners' sugar and beat for 2 minutes, until well combined. Add the vanilla and combine. In a separate bowl, combine the flour and salt, then add to the butter mixture. Mix until the dough sticks together when pinched. Fold the Halloween candy into the dough with a spatula.

3. Roll the dough out on a floured surface to ¼ inch-thick. Cut out cookies with your favorite Halloween cookie cutter. Place them on your prepared baking sheet and bake for 13 to 15 minutes. Cool completely, then enjoy!

Living Dead Cherry Berry Crumble

SERVES 6-8

Fruit crumble is the perfect fall recipe, so I'm thrilled to bring you a Halloween-y version! I used a life-size mold to create chocolate fingers and a hand, then filled it with my favorite lemon curd recipe, aka Edible Slime (page 109). The chocolate and lemon curd waken up your palette when eaten with a scoop of the crumble. What's coolest is that the fingers will soften when placed into the crumble dish, so it'll look like the zombie fingers are breaking apart as you scoop. So spooky!

Hand and Fingers:
2 cups total green, black, and white candy melts
Edible Slime (page 109)

Crumble:
¾ cup sugar
¼ cup cornstarch
½ teaspoon salt
6 cups frozen berry and cherry mix
Juice from ½ lemon
6 tablespoons unsalted butter, room temperature
¼ cup brown sugar
1 cup all-purpose flour
1 teaspoon cinnamon
½ teaspoon salt

Make the Zombie Hands and Fingers:

1. Place the green, black, and white candy melts in individual microwave-safe bowls and microwave for 30-second intervals until melted, stirring at each interval.

2. Spread the candy melts onto the inside of a life-size hand mold and a set of 5 fingers mold. You can swirl the 3 colors together, or paint details onto the hands. Be sure to fully coat the insides of the molds, as this shell will hold the filling. Place the molds in the refrigerator until the candy melts have set, about 30 minutes.

3. Fill the hand and fingers with the edible slime and pour more candy melts on top, sealing the slime inside.

4. Return the molds to the refrigerator to chill for at least 1 hour, or until the crumble is ready to eat.

Make the Crumble:

1. Preheat oven to 375°F. Place the sugar, cornstarch, and salt in a large bowl. Mix, then add the frozen berries and lemon juice and mix until well incorporated. Set aside.

2. Place the butter and brown sugar into a bowl and beat with an electric mixer until light and fluffy. Add the flour, cinnamon, and salt and mix with your hands, squeezing the mixture together to form lumps.

(Continued on next page)

3. Pour the berry filling into an 8×8-inch baking dish and scatter the crumble topping on top.

4. Bake for 50 to 60 minutes, until the juices are bubbling. Loosely cover the crumble with a sheet of aluminum foil at the 30-minute mark.

Assembly:
1. Once the crumble has baked, allow it to slightly cool for 15 to 20 minutes.

2. Stick the fingers and hand into the crumble. The heat of the crumble will soften the fingers, so once you place them in the crumble, it will be difficult to rearrange them—be careful!

3. To serve, take a scoop of the crumble along with a finger or piece of a hand!

Gummy Eyeballs

MAKES ABOUT 48 (1-INCH) EYEBALLS

Such a fun, fabulous treat to make for the holidays! These eyeballs are quite bouncy and work great as a cake or cupcake topping, floating in a drink, or eaten as is! I used a spherical ice cube tray to create perfectly spherical eyes that were about 1 inch in diameter. You could also use a jumbo ice cube mold to create giant eyes to float in your punch bowl.

Iris and Pupils:
2 tablespoons powdered gelatin
¼ cup + 1 tablespoon water
¾ cup cream soda, or any clear soda
Vanilla extract
Black, brown, green, blue, and red food
  coloring

White of the Eye:
1 cup water
½ cup powdered gelatin
1 cup condensed milk
¼ cup sugar
Vanilla extract

Make the Iris and Pupils:

1. Combine the gelatin and water in a microwave-safe cup. Heat for 20 to 30 seconds, until liquid.

2. Pour the cream soda, gelatin mixture, and 1 drop of vanilla into a small pot and set to medium heat. Heat until the gelatin has fully dissolved, then remove the pot from the heat.

3. Use a spoon to remove any foam that has accumulated on the surface and discard. Pour ¼ cup of the gelatin mixture into a small bowl. Dye it black with a couple drops of black food coloring.

4. Use a small spoon to drop 2 to 3 drops of black jelly into each space of a 1-inch sphere ice cube mold. Allow the pupils to set at room temperature while you make the iris.

5. Divide the remaining jelly into 4 bowls and dye one each brown, green, blue, and red. Use a small spoon to pour just enough iris jelly on top of the pupils so that you can see a ring of color around the pupil.

6. Leave the jelly to set at room temperature for 1 to 2 hours before making the white of the eye.

(Continued on page 99)

Make the White of the Eye:

1. Place the water and gelatin into a microwave-safe bowl. Microwave for 20-second intervals until liquid. Keep an eye on it, as the gelatin can bubble and create quite a mess in the microwave!

2. Pour the condensed milk, sugar, a drop of vanilla, and the gelatin mixture into a small pot and set it to medium heat. Mix until the gelatin has dissolved and everything is fully incorporated. Use a spoon to remove any foam that has accumulated on the surface and discard.

3. Pour the mixture into the molds and place the lid on top. Place the mold in the refrigerator overnight, or until the gummy mixture has fully set.

4. Gently unmold the eyes and enjoy!

DIY Pumpkin Spice Mix

MAKES ABOUT 5 TEASPOONS

For those of you who don't have access to premixed pumpkin pie spice—this recipe is an essential! Make a big batch and use it all season long for cakes, cookies, homemade pumpkin spice lattes, and way more. It can be stored at room temperature in your cupboard in a spice jar.

3 teaspoons ground cinnamon
¾ teaspoon ground nutmeg
¾ teaspoon ground ginger
Rounded ¼ teaspoon ground cloves

1. Mix all spices and enjoy!

CREEPY CANDY

SPIDERWEB MARSHMALLOWS

MAKES ABOUT 12 MARSHMALLOWS

Homemade marshmallows are leaps and bounds better than store-bought. Imagine a fluffy vanilla cloud, made in the comfort of your house! Once the marshmallow mixture is made, you do have to work quickly to pipe out the marshmallows before it begins to set, so if you are baking with your little ones, I recommend that you handle the piping and allow them to take charge of dusting the marshmallows with the sugar powder.

⅓ cup + ¼ cup cold water, divided
2½ teaspoons powdered gelatin
1 cup sugar
½ vanilla bean pod (seeds only), or ½ teaspoon vanilla extract
Cornstarch

1. Draw circles onto a sheet of parchment paper using the rim of your desired mug. This will ensure that the marshmallows will fit into your cup. Draw spiderwebs inside the circles. Flip the sheet of parchment paper over and place on a baking sheet.

2. Pour ⅓ cup of cold water into the bowl of an electric mixer and sprinkle the powdered gelatin on top. Let sit for 5 minutes.

3. Place the sugar and ¼ cup cold water in a small pot and set to medium-high heat. Stir until the sugar has melted.

4. Attach a candy thermometer to the pot and boil the sugar until it reaches 238°F. Brush the sides of the pot with a wet pastry brush if sugar crystals stick to the sides.

5. Add the hot sugar to the gelatin and stir the mixture by hand, whisking for a few minutes to slightly cool. Then beat with an electric mixer on medium-high speed for 8 to 10 minutes, until soft peaks form. Then add the vanilla bean seeds and mix well.

6. Place the marshmallow in a piping bag fitted with a narrow round tip. Pipe the marshmallows following the lines on the parchment paper. Work quickly, as the marshmallow will begin to stiffen. Let the marshmallows set for 1 hour.

7. Dust the marshmallows with cornstarch and gently peel them off the parchment paper. Flip them over and dust the undersides with cornstarch. Bounce them in a sieve to remove any excess cornstarch and enjoy! To store, place them in a single layer in a zip-top bag.

Marshmallow Ghosts

MAKES ABOUT 12 (2-INCH) GHOSTS

Homemade marshmallows taste exquisite. They are so soft, pillowy, and delicious. These marshmallows are best consumed within 1 to 2 days of making them. To store them, place them in a sealed plastic container or sandwich bag and add an extra sprinkle of the sugar coating from step 7.

⅓ + ¼ **cup cold water, divided**
2½ **teaspoons powdered gelatin**
1 **cup sugar**
Seeds from 1 vanilla bean, or
  1 **teaspoon vanilla extract**
¼ **cup mini chocolate chips**
¼ **cup confectioners' sugar**
¼ **cup cornstarch**

1. Pour ⅓ cup of cold water into the bowl of an electric mixer and sprinkle the powdered gelatin on top. Let sit for 5 minutes.

2. Place the sugar and ¼ cup cold water in a small pot and set to medium-high heat. Stir until the sugar has melted.

3. Attach a candy thermometer to the pot and boil the sugar until it reaches 238°F. Brush the sides of the pot with a wet pastry brush if sugar crystals stick to the sides. Remove the pot from the heat and stir until the sugar stops boiling.

4. Add the hot sugar to the gelatin and stir the mixture by hand whisking for a few minutes to slightly cool. Then beat with an electric mixer on medium-high speed for 8 to 10 minutes, until soft peaks form. Add the vanilla bean seeds and mix until combined.

5. Place the marshmallow mixture in a piping bag fitted with a large, round piping tip. Line a baking sheet with parchment paper and pipe tall swirls onto the paper. Stick 2 mini chocolate chips onto each marshmallow as the eyes.

6. Allow the marshmallow to stiffen at room temperature for 6 hours, or overnight, until firm to the touch.

7. Combine the confectioners' sugar and cornstarch in a bowl and place in a mesh sieve. Dust over the surface of the marshmallow. Remove the marshmallows from the pan with a butter knife and dust the underside of the marshmallows with the sugar coating.

8. Bounce in a mesh sieve to remove any excess coating and enjoy! These are best consumed within 24 hours.

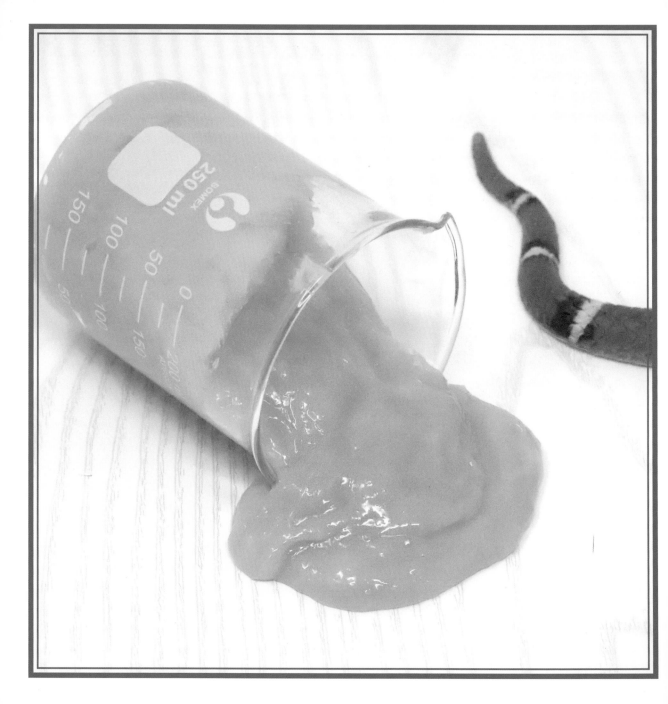

Edible Slime

This slime is perfect for so many Halloween recipes! Use it as a cupcake filling, as zombie goo for my Living Dead Cherry Berry Crumble (page 95), or even fill truffles with it!

3 large eggs
1 cup granulated sugar
½ cup fresh lemon juice (about 3 lemons)
¼ cup unsalted butter, cold and cut into cubes
Zest from 2 lemons
Green food coloring

1. Place a pot over medium heat and add the eggs, sugar, and lemon juice. Whisk until blended, then add the butter and lemon zest.

2. Cook, whisking constantly, until the mixture has thickened and coats the back of a spoon.

3. Transfer to a bowl and cool for 10 minutes. Dye the slime your desired shade of green with food coloring.

4. Cover with plastic wrap and chill in the refrigerator until cold. Enjoy!

Red Blood Cell Dumplings

MAKES 15-20 DUMPLINGS

In another life I would absolutely have been a doctor, so I decided to mesh these lives together for this recipe and create red blood cell dumplings! These dumplings are made with a variety of rice flour called shiratamako. It can be found online and in specialty grocery stores.

⅔ cup shiratamako rice flour
⅓ cup + 1 tablespoon water
Red food coloring
½ cup coconut cream
1½ tablespoons light brown sugar
½ cup raspberries

1. First, make the dumplings. Place the shiratamako flour into a bowl and gradually drizzle in the water. Knead with a spoon (or your hands, which is much easier). The dough should form into one piece and be firm enough for a piece of dough to be rolled into a ball, and retain its form when placed down. Depending on the humidity of your house, you may need to add a bit more flour or water, but do so very gradually.

2. Dye the dough red with some food coloring.

3. Roll the dough into 15 to 20 little balls, then flatten them with your hands and press a small indentation into each to create red blood cell shapes!

4. Place the dumplings in a pot of boiling water. Once they have risen to the surface, boil for 1 minute, then remove and place in a bowl of ice water to stop the cooking. Move them onto a plate lined with plastic wrap while you make the syrup.

5. Place the coconut cream, brown sugar, and raspberries into a pan and bring to a boil. Boil for about 3 minutes, until everything comes together and the raspberries infuse into the cream. Add some red food coloring to make it look like blood. Pour this through a cheesecloth to remove the raspberry seeds.

6. Spoon the red blood cells into a bowl, then pour the blood syrup on top. Enjoy!

GIANT CRISPY RICE PUMPKIN

MAKES A 9-INCH PUMPKIN

Homemade rice treats are some of my favorite treats to make. They taste worlds better than the store-bought version and can be molded into any shape imaginable!

Brown Center:
½ cup margarine or butter
10 cups marshmallows
1 teaspoon vanilla extract
1 cup dark or milk chocolate chips
12 cups crispy rice cereal
Cooking spray

Orange Shell:
½ cup margarine or butter
10 cups marshmallows
1 teaspoon vanilla extract
Orange food coloring
12 cups crispy rice cereal
Cooking spray

Make the Center:

1. In a microwave safe bowl, microwave the margarine for 30 to 60 seconds or until melted. Add the marshmallows, vanilla, and chocolate chips, mix to combine, then microwave for 1 to 1½ minutes, stopping halfway to stir. Heat until melted and smooth when stirred.

2. Add the rice cereal and stir until well combined.

3. Reserve ½ cup of this mixture. Spray your hands with cooking spray and shape the remaining portion into ball. Shape the smaller amount into the stem, but do not attach to the main piece. Wrap both pieces in plastic wrap and place in the refrigerator to chill.

Make the Orange Shell:

1. In a microwave-safe bowl, microwave the margarine for 30 to 60 seconds or until melted. Add the marshmallows and vanilla, mix to combine, then microwave for 1 to 1½ minutes, stopping halfway to stir. Heat until melted and smooth when stirred.

2. Dye the mixture orange with the food coloring. Add the rice cereal and stir until well combined.

3. Lay a large sheet of plastic wrap onto your work surface and spray with cooking spray. Place the rice cereal on top, spray again with cooking spray, and place another sheet of plastic wrap on top. Use a rolling pin to flatten to about ½-inch thick. Remove the top sheet of plastic wrap, then wrap the orange layer completely around the brown layer.

4. Once the brown layer is fully covered, place the pumpkin on your work surface and place the stem on top. Cover in plastic wrap and return to the refrigerator overnight to chill and stiffen.

5. Use a sharp knife to carve a jack-o'-lantern face out of the pumpkin, peeling off just the orange layer. Serve and enjoy!

BLEEDING HEART PANNA COTTA

MAKES 2 HEARTS

Panna cotta is such an underrated dessert. It's pudding's fancier cousin and I could eat it all day! I used a life-size heart mold to create this panna cotta, which is drizzled with homemade syrup. For an extra flavorful touch, add some fresh strawberries to the syrup while simmering.

Panna Cotta Hearts:

6 tablespoons cold water

7 teaspoons powdered gelatin

3 cups heavy cream

¾ cup sugar

1 cup whole milk

Red food coloring

Blood Syrup:

1½ cups water (or dark red juice)

Dark red or burgundy food coloring

½ cup sugar

1 teaspoon vanilla extract (or 1 vanilla bean + seeds)

Make the Hearts:

1. Pour the cold water into a large bowl and sprinkle the gelatin on top. Let sit for 5 minutes.

2. Pour the cream and sugar into a medium-sized pot and set to medium-high heat. Stir to dissolve the sugar and heat until the mixture starts to bubble. Remove from the heat and add to the gelatin. Whisk to combine.

3. Add the milk and enough red food coloring to reach your desired shade. Whisk to combine. Pour the mixture through a sieve.

4. Set the heart-shaped molds into bowls to keep them level, then fill the molds with the panna cotta. Place in the refrigerator and chill overnight, until the panna cotta has set.

Make the Syrup:

1. Dye the water a deep red with some food coloring. Pour the water, sugar, and vanilla into a small pot, set to medium-high heat.

2. Bring the mixture to a boil, stirring to dissolve the sugar. Reduce the heat to medium-low and simmer for 25 to 30 minutes, until the syrup reduces to about ½ cup. Remove from the heat and cool for 5 minutes, then transfer to a jug to serve.

3. Turn the hearts out onto serving plates. If the panna cotta is sticking to the molds, wrap a warm, damp dishcloth around the molds to slightly warm the mold.

4. Pour the bloody syrup on top and enjoy!

BRAIN PUDDING

MAKES 1 BRAIN

This brain pudding has a spooky filling inside! Slice open to reveal a strawberry cream center!

2 packets strawberry banana Jell-O
1 tablespoon + 3 teaspoons powdered
  gelatin, divided
2 cups boiling water
2 cups cold water
½ cup milk
1 dozen strawberries
½ cup whipping cream
¼ cup sugar

1. Combine the Jell-O and 1 tablespoon plain powdered gelatin in a bowl. Add the boiling water and mix until the powder has fully dissolved.

2. Add the cold water and fully combine. Place a brain-shaped mold into a bowl (for stability) and pour in the mixture. Place it in the refrigerator until fully set, about 3 to 4 hours.

3. Pour the milk into a small pot and set to medium heat. Gradually sprinkle in the 3 teaspoons gelatin, whisking with each addition until it is fully combined.

4. Pour this milk along with the strawberries, whipping cream, and sugar into a blender and pulse until smooth.

5. Scoop the center of the brain out of the mold, and pour the mousse inside. Return the mold to the refrigerator to fully set, about 4 hours.

6. To unmold the brain, run a warm, wet dishcloth over the mold and turn it out onto a plate. Slice to reveal the soft center!

Blood Clot Lollipops

MAKES ABOUT 12 LOLLIPOPS

The perfect treat for spooky gifting—wrap them individually in cellophane for a fun and unique take on Halloween candy!

2½ cups granulated sugar
1 cup water
1½ cups light corn syrup
1–2 drops of your desired flavoring
Cooking spray
Red food coloring
Toothpicks
Lollipop sticks

1. Place a pot over medium heat and add the sugar, water, and light corn syrup. Stir with a rubber spatula until everything is melted and combined. Increase the heat to medium-high, attach a candy thermometer to the pot, and heat until the sugar reaches 310°F.

2. Remove the pot from the heat and stir until it stops bubbling. Add the flavoring and mix until fully combined.

3. Generously spray a lollipop mold with cooking spray. Working with one mold at a time, pour some candy into the mold and add a few drops of red food coloring on top. Swirl the food coloring with a toothpick, then insert a lollipop stick. Repeat with the remaining candy and molds.

4. Allow the lollipops to cool at room temperature for 1 hour, or until fully hardened. Unmold and enjoy!

CANDY CORN JELLIES

MAKES ABOUT 18 JELLIES

If you're a fan of candy corn, this recipe is for you! These jellies are adorable and striped just like the famous candy. If you're of drinking age, replace the milk in the candy corn milk recipe with vodka or tequila!

Candy Corn Milk:
1 cup candy corn
4 cups milk

Jellies:
Cooking spray
1½ cups + ¾ cup water, divided
6 tablespoons powdered gelatin
1 cup condensed milk
1 cup milk
1 cup candy corn milk (recipe below)
1 teaspoon vanilla extract
Yellow and orange food coloring
Whipped cream
Candy corn pieces, for garnish

Make the Candy Corn Milk:

1. Pour the candy corn into your desired container, until the container is roughly ⅓ full.

2. Fill the rest of the way with milk, seal, give it a stir, then place in the refrigerator overnight for the milk to infuse.

Make the Jellies:

1. Spray a 9×9 inch pan with cooking spray. Set aside.

2. Pour 1½ cups water into a pot and sprinkle the gelatin on top. Allow the gelatin to develop for 5 minutes. Set the pot to medium heat and whisk constantly until the gelatin has dissolved and is liquid.

3. Remove the pot from the heat and add the condensed milk, whisking until fully combined. Add the plain milk, candy corn milk, and vanilla. Mix until combined.

4. Divide the mixture into 3 bowls. Leave one bowl white and dye the remaining bowls each yellow and orange.

5. Pour the white layer into the pan and place in the refrigerator for 20 to 30 minutes, or until firm to the touch. Repeat with the yellow layer and chill for 30 minutes. Pour the orange layer on top and chill for 2 hours.

6. Gently pull the sides of the jelly away from the pan with your fingertips, then invert it onto a plate, and slice into squares.

7. If desired, top with whipped cream and candy corn, or just leave bare. Enjoy!

Pumpkin Dumplings

MAKES 9 PUMPKINS; FILLS 3 SKEWERS

Mitarashi dango are a classic Japanese soft rice ball recipe with a sweet soy sauce glaze. For the uninitiated, imagine deep, brown caramel. Removed from the stove just before it gets too caramelized and bitter. Mitarashi sauce tastes similar, with slightly less sweetness. These rice balls are also known as mochi and are made with a specific kind of rice flour, called shiratamako. It can be found online or in specialty grocery stores.

3½ ounces canned pumpkin
1 teaspoon pumpkin pie spice
1½ ounces shiratamako rice flour
Cocoa powder
½ cup water
3 tablespoons sugar
1 tablespoon soy sauce
2 teaspoons potato starch
3 bamboo skewers

1. Place the pumpkin in a microwave-safe bowl and microwave for 30 seconds, or until warm.

2. Add the pumpkin pie spice and shiratamako flour and mix until fully combined.

3. Take a small piece of dough and knead it together with some cocoa powder to dye it brown. Divide the remaining dough into 9 balls. Make grooves around the sides with a skewer to create pumpkin shapes.

4. Divide the brown dough into 9 pieces and shape them into small stems. Stick one onto each pumpkin.

5. Place the pumpkins in a pot of boiling water, and once they rise to the surface, boil for 1 minute. Place them into a bowl of ice water to stop the cooking. Set aside.

6. For the sauce, place the water, sugar, soy sauce, and potato starch into a small pot set to medium heat. Heat until the sauce has thickened.

7. Skewer 3 pumpkins onto each skewer and coat in the mitarashi sauce.

Toad Eye Pudding

MAKES ABOUT 3 CUPS

This is a coconut cream pudding and is loved by my entire household, including my dogs, who snuck some while I was shooting this recipe and had my back turned. I am envious of those who get to try this recipe, because mine unfortunately was tainted by Pomeranian tongues.

½ cup granulated sugar
3 tablespoons cornstarch
Pinch of salt
2 large egg yolks
½ cup heavy cream
1½ cups coconut cream
½ teaspoon vanilla extract
½ teaspoon coconut extract
2 tablespoons unsalted butter
Green and yellow food coloring
10 cups water
2 cups quick-cooking tapioca pearls

Make the Pudding:

1. Pour the sugar, cornstarch, and salt into a pot. Whisk to combine. Add the egg yolks and heavy cream and whisk until well combined. Add the coconut cream and mix well.

2. Set the pot to medium-high heat and whisk constantly for 5 to 10 minutes, until the mixture has thickened and is bubbling.

3. Pour the pudding through a sieve, then add the vanilla, coconut extract, and butter, whisking until well combined. Add some green and yellow food coloring to create a lime color.

4. Press a sheet of plastic wrap onto the surface of the pudding and place in the refrigerator until chilled, about 3 hours.

Cook the Tapioca:

1. Fill a large pot with 10 cups of water and bring to a boil. Add the tapioca and stir gently.

2. Once the tapioca floats to the surface, cover and reduce to medium heat. Boil for 2 to 3 minutes, then turn off the heat and simmer for an additional 2 to 3 minutes.

3. Drain and place the tapioca in cold water for 1 minute, to stop the cooking.

4. Drain again and mix the tapioca with the pudding. Serve!

Petri Dish Treats

FILLS 12 PETRI DISHES

These treats use aloe juice as a base. Aloe juice is one of my favorites and usually comes with packed with juicy aloe pulp, which adds dimension to these petri dish treats and makes it look like there is something mysterious floating in the jelly.

3 tablespoons powdered gelatin

¼ cup water

2 cups aloe juice (I get mine at an Asian grocery store)

Candy and sprinkles

Blue, red, yellow, and green food coloring

1. Combine the gelatin and water in a microwave-safe bowl. Microwave for 15-second intervals, until the gelatin has melted.

2. Combine the gelatin mixture and aloe juice and whisk until combined.

3. Divide this between 12 new and clean petri dishes.

4. Before the jelly has set, place candies and sprinkles into the petri dishes. For a mold-like effect, drop tiny drops of food coloring into the dishes. The color will feather at the edges and look very cool!

5. Transfer the petri dishes to the refrigerator to chill for 1 hour, or until the jelly has set.

6. Serve and enjoy!

EDIBLE BLOOD

MAKES ABOUT ½ CUP

A classic and necessary recipe for any Halloween baker! Cornstarch is used to thicken the blood, so use more or less depending on how runny you would like your blood to be.

½ cup clear corn syrup
2 teaspoons cornstarch
Red food coloring
Blue food coloring

1. Combine the corn syrup and cornstarch in a bowl. The cornstarch will thicken the blood, so add as little or as much as you like!

2. Add enough red food coloring to achieve a deep red shade. Add the tiniest amount of blue food coloring—around ¼ of a drop. This will add depth to the red, but not make it turn purple.

3. Apply to your desired cake, candies, or cookies! To store, simply place in a sealed plastic container and store in the refrigerator.

Classic Candy Apples

COATS ABOUT 12 APPLES

It's important that you thoroughly wash the apples before starting. They are usually coated in wax, which will prevent the candy coating from sticking. I've found that splashing some white vinegar on my hands as I'm washing them really helps remove the waxy feeling. For an extra-special touch, brush the candy apples with edible glitter once cooled. They'll look beautiful!

4½ cups granulated sugar
1½ cups water
¾ cups corn syrup
12 Granny Smith apples
Lollipop sticks or skewers
Cooking spray
Red food coloring

1. Place the granulated, water, and corn syrup into a medium-sized pot and stir to combine.

2. Set to medium-high heat and attach a candy thermometer. Heat to 302°F.

3. In the meantime, wash the apples, remove the stems, and insert lollipop sticks or skewers into the top. Spray a baking sheet with cooking spray and set aside.

4. Once the candy reaches 302°F, remove the pot from the heat. Add several drops of red food coloring to achieve your desired color.

5. Dip the apples into the candy coating, then place on the baking sheet. Cool completely and enjoy!

CARAMEL APPLES

MAKES 6 APPLES

These classic caramel apples are dipped in soft, creamy vanilla caramel. If you're not a huge fan of candy apples with the hard candy coating, this is the recipe for you!

Long lollipop sticks
6 Granny Smith apples
14 ounces soft caramel candies
2 tablespoons milk

1. Stick the lollipop sticks into the top of the apples, and place them onto a baking sheet lined with parchment paper.

2. Place the caramels and milk into a pot and set to medium heat. Keep stirring until the candies have fully melted.

3. Dip each apple into the caramel sauce, and fully coat it. Then place them on the baking sheet to set. If any bubbles appear on the caramel, simply poke them with a sharp knife and deflate them.

BLACK POISON APPLES

MAKES 6 APPLES

My favorite candy apple recipe in this book! We're taking the Classic Caramel Apples and dunking them in chocolate. Chocolate and caramel are a fantastic combination, but the tartness of the green apple cuts through the sweetness and tastes amazing. This is one recipe that I gladly make on repeat and feel no shame in indulging in. When eating, I recommend slicing it into wedges. It's far easier than trying to take bites of the entire apple!

Long lollipop sticks
6 Granny Smith apples
14 ounces soft caramel candies
2 tablespoons milk
2 cups milk or dark chocolate
   chips
2 cups black sugar

1. Stick the lollipop sticks into the top of the apples and place them onto a baking sheet lined with parchment paper.

2. Place the caramels and milk into a pot and set to medium heat. Keep stirring until the candies have fully melted.

3. Dip each apple into the caramel sauce, and fully coat it. Then place them on the baking sheet to set. If any bubbles appear on the caramel, simply poke them with a sharp knife and deflate them.

4. Once the caramel has cooled and fully set, it's time to make the chocolate topping! Place the candy apples on a plate lined with parchment paper and chill them in the refrigerator while you make the topping. The cool surface of the apples will set the candy melts at a quicker pace and make the black sugar stick better.

5. Place the chocolate chips in a microwave-safe bowl and microwave at 30-second intervals until melted, stirring at each interval. Prepare the black sugar in a bowl and place next to the candy melts.

6. Working with one apple at a time, dip it into the chocolate, rotating the apple until all of the caramel is covered. Gently remove any excess chocolate from the apple by wiping the base of the apple against the edge of the bowl. While the chocolate is still wet, dunk the apple into the black sugar and fully coat. I found that placing the apple in the middle of the sugar bowl and spooning the sugar onto the apple was the easiest for me.

7. Return the apples to the refrigerator to chill for 30 minutes until set, then enjoy!

Rainbow Candy Apples

MAKES ABOUT 2 APPLES PER COLOR (ABOUT 12 APPLES)

You'll see throughout this book that there is a grand total of 4 (!) candy apple recipes. I wanted to narrow it down, but at the same time, I couldn't leave you hanging in a time of the year where apples are just begging to be eaten. These candy apples are next level because they are also rainbow! The just exude happiness, don't they? If you plan on making all colors, be sure to make them in the order I suggest in the instructions. That way you'll only have to wash the pan 3 times instead of 6!

4½ cups granulated sugar
1½ cups water
¾ cup corn syrup
3 tablespoons white food coloring
Food coloring in any colors you prefer
12 Granny Smith apples
Lollipop sticks or skewers
Cooking spray

1. You will be making 2 colors per batch, so just repeat these steps 3 times. Place 1½ cups granulated sugar, ½ cup water, and ¼ cup corn syrup into a medium-sized pot and stir to combine. Add 1 tablespoon white food coloring and several drops pink food coloring and mix well.

2. Set to medium-high heat and attach a candy thermometer. Heat to 302°F.

3. In the meantime, wash the apples, remove the stems, and insert lollipop sticks or skewers into the top. Spray a baking sheet with cooking spray and set aside.

4. Once the candy reaches 302°F, dip 2 apples into the pink candy, then place on the baking sheet. Add some orange food coloring to the candy, mix well, then coat 2 apples in orange candy.

5. To easily clean the pot between batches, pour out any excess candy into a silicone mold, then fill the pot with water. Bring to a boil and boil until the excess candy coating melts. Pour out the hot water, then repeat steps 1–4, making yellow and green in one batch and blue and purple in the last batch.

Body Part Dog Treats

MAKES ABOUT 2 CUPS JELLY MIXTURE, WHICH CAN BE POURED INTO ANY MOLD YOU LIKE!

We can't leave out our puppies at Halloween! Serve a platter of brains to your pups and watch them embrace their inner zombie!

Olive oil

White Base:

½ cup plain 2% unsweetened Greek yogurt

½ cup water, divided

2 tablespoons plain powdered gelatin (*not* Jell-O)

6 tablespoons beef stock (must be dog safe, without onions and garlic)

Pink Top:

1 cup frozen strawberries (*not* raspberries—they can be toxic for dogs in large quantities), thawed

2 tablespoons plain powdered gelatin (*not* Jell-O)

6 tablespoons beef stock (must be dog safe, without onions and garlic)

1. Lightly coat the insides of a teeth or brain mold with olive oil.

2. Make the white base. Combine the yogurt and ¼ cup water in a bowl. Set aside. Combine the gelatin and beef stock in a small bowl and microwave for 15 to 30 seconds, or until the gelatin has melted. Add this to the yogurt mixture and mix to combine. Set aside.

3. For the pink layer, place the strawberries in a food processor and pulse until completely liquid. Combine the gelatin and beef stock in a small bowl and microwave for 15 to 30 seconds, or until the gelatin has melted. Add the gelatin mixture to the juice and mix well. Set aside.

4. To make a teeth, pour the white mixture into a teeth mold to fill it about halfway. Place it in the refrigerator for 5 minutes, or until the jelly has just partially set—this is important! It should be sticky like jam. Then fill the mold the rest of the way with the strawberry mixture.

5. To make the brain, pour the strawberry mixture into a brain mold and place it in the refrigerator for 10 minutes, or until just partially set. Pour the yogurt mixture on top of the strawberry mixture. If you'd like more of an ombre effect, use a straw or toothpick to slightly swirl the yogurt into the strawberry. If your brain mold isn't full, whip up another batch of the strawberry or yogurt mixture and pour it on top. You can even add a couple whole strawberries!

6. Return the mold to the refrigerator and chill for 45 minutes. Then unmold and give to your doggy! To help unmold the jellies, you can dunk the base of the mold into a tray filled with hot water for a couple seconds. Don't leave it in too long or it will melt!

Bloody PB&J Cups

MAKES ABOUT 6 CUPS

Homemade peanut butter cups are so much fun, even more so when they're filled with jam and peanut butter chips and topped with super realistic candy glass! Bite into a cup and taste the delicious bloody raspberry jam ooze out.

Broken Glass Candy:
1¼ cups granulated sugar
½ cup water
¾ cup light corn syrup

PB&J Cups:
2 cups white candy melts or white chocolate
6 cupcake liners (paper or silicone work, but silicone are preferable)
¼ cup peanut butter chips
6 tablespoons raspberry jam

Edible Blood (page 129)

Make the Broken Glass:

1. Place a pot over medium heat, and add the granulated sugar, water, and light corn syrup. Stir with a rubber spatula until everything is melted and combined.

2. Then increase the heat to medium-high, and attach a candy thermometer to the pot. Heat the sugar until it reaches 310°F, remove from the heat, and mix until it stops bubbling.

3. Pour the mixture onto a baking sheet lined with a Silpat mat or a sheet of parchment paper greased with cooking spray. Smooth the surface with a rubber spatula and allow the candy to cool at room temperature for 3 to 4 hours, until cooled completely.

4. Use a spoon to carefully break the candy into pieces to look like glass shards! This candy is sharp, so be careful when handling. If making this candy ahead of time, store in a zip-top bag.

Make the Cups:

1. Place the white candy melts into a microwave-safe bowl. Microwave for 30-second intervals until melted, mixing at each interval.

2. Place 6 cupcake liners onto a tray. Pour enough candy melts into the cupcake liners to just cover the base. Place the tray of cupcake liners into the refrigerator until the candy melts have set, about 15 minutes. Return the cupcake liners to your work surface and spread more candy melts up the sides of the cupcake liners and a little more on the base. Here we are creating the bottom and sides of the cups. You don't want them to be too thick, but also not too thin that they will break when unmolding later.

(Continued on next page)

3. Sprinkle the peanut butter chips into the cups, about 2 teaspoons per cup, and return the cups to the refrigerator for 15 to 20 minutes, until the candy melts have set.

4. Divide the raspberry jam between the cups. Keep a clean perimeter of candy melts around the jam to ensure it doesn't leak out the sides. Pour the remaining candy melts around and on top of the jam. Stick some of the broken glass candy into the melted candy melts and the jam filling.

5. Return the cups to the refrigerator and chill for 1 to 2 hours, until the cups are firm.

6. Unmold the cups and arrange them on the platter of your choice. When ready to serve, spoon some Edible Blood onto the tips of the candy glass and watch it drip down!

DRINKS

PUMPKIN JUICE

SERVES 8-10

This sweet, sparkling pumpkin juice is a very fun and unique Halloween drink. Serve it in a pumpkin-shaped punch bowl for an extra festive touch!

1½ cups pure pumpkin puree (not pumpkin pie filling)
1 cup apricot juice
1½ cups cream soda
2 cups apple cider (non-alcoholic)
1½ cups ginger ale
Ice (optional, I didn't use it)

1. Combine the pumpkin puree and apricot juice in a bowl or large measuring cup. Pour through a cheesecloth into a pumpkin cauldron.

2. Add the cream soda, apple cider, ginger ale, and ice, if using, and mix. Enjoy!

Bloody Syringes

FILLS 30-45 SYRINGES

Although a vampire may disagree, theses strawberry lemonade bloody syringes are much more palatable than the real deal. If you are of drinking age, you can replace the lemonade with tequila, vodka, or whatever you like!

1 cup water
1 cup granulated sugar
2 cups chopped strawberries
½ cup lemonade

1. Pour the water and sugar into a pot and set to medium-high heat. Stir until the sugar has dissolved, then add the strawberries and boil for 10 minutes. Reduce the heat to medium-low and simmer for 10 more minutes.

2. Strain the syrup through a mesh sieve to remove the strawberry pieces. Place in the refrigerator and cool completely.

3. Mix the syrup and lemonade, then draw the drink into the syringes. When shopping for syringes to use, use oral syringes, as they don't have a needle attached and have a larger opening.

4. Serve on a flat tray, or in a glass, with the openings pointing downward. Enjoy!

Magical Potion

MAKES ABOUT 2 LITERS

This potion is so simple to whip up, but packs a punch! For an extra-special touch, serve it in a cauldron!

2 cans frozen limeade
Water
4 cups (1 liter) Sprite
Green food coloring (optional)
Silver sugar stars

1. Pour the limeade into a bowl. Add 4 cans' worth of water into the bowl. Add the Sprite.

2. Add some green food coloring, if using.

3. Stir, then pour into vials. Top with silver stars and enjoy!

Sparkling Unicorn Blood

MAKES 2 CUPS

Unicorns are magical beings who have sparkly purple and delicious blood! Get your spooky on and indulge in this mystical essence!

1 cup cream soda
1 cup pineapple juice
2 tablespoons freeze-dried raspberry
   powder, or ½ cup mashed raspberries,
   strained and seeds removed
Purple food coloring
1 tablespoon pink pearl dust
1 tablespoon purple pearl dust

1. Combine the cream soda, pineapple juice, and freeze-dried raspberries in a bowl. Whisk until everything is fully incorporated.

2. Add 1 or 2 drops of purple food coloring and both pink and purple pearl dust.

3. Use a funnel to pour it into test tubes. Before serving, give them a little stir to see the blood shimmer!

Specimen Jar Drinks

SERVES 6-8

These are so much fun! You can use any mold shape you have on hand to create the specimens, and if you're of drinking age, replace the grape juice in the specimens and the lemonade in the cocktails with vodka or tequila!

Specimen:
Cooking spray
1½ cups + ¾ cup water, divided
6 tablespoons gelatin
1 cup sweetened condensed milk
1 cup milk
1 cup grape juice
1 teaspoon vanilla extract
Food coloring

Cocktails:
2 cups lemonade
2 cups Sprite
2 cups soda water

1. Spray your molds with cooking spray. We used skulls, brains, pigs, frogs, and bones. Set aside.

2. Pour 1½ cups water into a pot and sprinkle the gelatin on top. Allow the gelatin to develop for 5 minutes. Set the pot to medium heat and whisk constantly until the gelatin has dissolved and is liquid. Remove the pot from the heat and add the sweetened condensed milk, whisking to combine. Add the milk, grape juice, vanilla, and ¾ cup water and whisk until fully combined.

3. Divide the mixture into bowls and dye them your desired colors.

4. Pour into the molds, then transfer the molds to the refrigerator to set, about 1 hour.

5. In a large jug, combine the lemonade, Sprite, and soda water.

6. Unmold the specimens and place them in small mason jars. Fill with the cocktail, seal, and serve!

GLOW-IN-THE-DARK WITCH'S BREW

MAKES ABOUT 2 LITERS

Tonic water is a fabulous ingredient that glows when placed under black light! I've adapted my favorite lemonade recipe to feature tonic water instead of sparkling water. Tonic water can have a distinctive taste, but don't worry if you're not a fan! The lemonade flavor wins out here.

1½ cups sugar
1 cup water
2½ cups freshly squeezed lemon juice
5 cups tonic water
Corn syrup, for garnish
Black edible glitter, for garnish

1. Bring the sugar and water to a boil in a pan over high heat. Stir until the sugar is dissolved, and allow to fully cool. You can refrigerate this to speed up the process, or do this the night before.

2. Add the lemon juice and tonic water to the sugar syrup and mix. If you find that it is too sweet, you can add up to 2 more cups of tonic water.

3. Refrigerate until chilled.

4. When ready to serve, coat the rims of glasses with corn syrup and dip them in black edible glitter. Pour the brew into the glasses and switch on a black light!

Shrunken Head Apple Cider

It's time to bob for apples! . . . Apple HEADS!

Apple Cider:
9 apples, cut into quarters (peel, seeds, and stems intact)

1 orange, cut into quarters (peel, seeds, and stems intact)

3 cinnamon sticks

3 teaspoons ground nutmeg (or 1 whole nutmeg)

1½ teaspoons ground cloves (or 2 teaspoons whole cloves)

½ teaspoon allspice

12–16 cups water

⅓ cup brown sugar

Shrunken Heads:
6 Granny Smith apples

2 cups lemon juice

2 tablespoons salt

Make the Apple Cider:
1. Place the apples and orange into a slow cooker. Add the cinnamon sticks, nutmeg, cloves, and allspice. Mix well and add the water, pouring until the slow cooker is almost full.

2. Cook on high heat for 3 to 4 hours or low heat for 6 to 8 hours.

3. An hour before the cider is finished, mash the softened apples and orange slices with a potato masher. Continue cooking for one more hour.

4. Strain the cider into a clean pot. Add the brown sugar and mix well.

Make the Shrunken Heads:
1. Preheat oven to 250°F and line a baking sheet with parchment paper.

2. Peel the apples and cut them in half through the stem. Remove the seeds and the core.Use a sharp paring knife to cut facial features into the rounded sides of the apples.

3. In a large bowl, combine the lemon juice and salt. Add the apples into the lemon juice mixture once they have been peeled and carved (this will prevent browning).

4. Once all apples have been carved, place them on your prepared baking sheet and bake for 90 minutes, until the apples are dry and are beginning to brown around the edges.

5. Once the cider is ready, add the apples and enjoy!

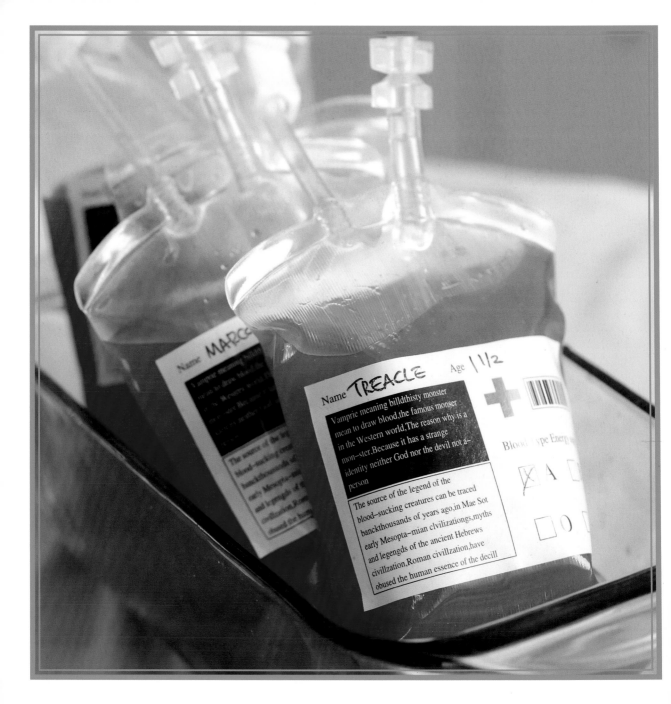

Blood Bag Drinks

FILLS 5 BLOOD BAGS

How cool are these?! I purchased these drink bags online and they delight me every time I open up my refrigerator. Hosting a spooky party? Hang these bags in your kitchen with your friends' names on them and have them find their bag!

4½ cups orange juice
½ cup grenadine
1 cup tequila (or lemonade)
Red food coloring

1. Combine all the ingredients in a bowl. If you would like virgin cocktails, simply omit the tequila!

2. Write your guests' names, ages, and blood types onto the blood bag labels with a black permanent marker. Stick to the blood bags.

3. Use the syringe that comes in the blood bag kit to squeeze the cocktails into the bags. The opening of the syringe is the same size as the tube, so you can use a small, round piping tip as a funnel! Just insert it into the tip of the tube and squeeze the syringe into the piping tip.

4. Enjoy your delicious blood!

Vampire Duck Hot Chocolate Bombs

Hot chocolate bombs are always such an amusing treat and these little vampire ducklings do not disappoint!

Duck Shells:
2 cups white candy melts
2 tablespoons black candy melts

Filling:
1½ cups high quality white
    chocolate, melted
¼ cup whipping cream
2 tablespoons raspberry jam
Red food coloring (optional)
1 cup of warm milk, per person

Make the Shells:
1. Place the white candy melts in a microwave-safe bowl and microwave for 30-second intervals until melted, stirring at each interval.

2. Spread the white chocolate onto the insides of a duck mold. Place the mold into the refrigerator until the candy melts have fully set.

Make the Filling:
1. Combine the melted white chocolate and whipping cream. Add the raspberry jam and red food coloring, if using, and mix well.

Assembly:
1. Fill the ducks with the filling. Be sure to leave a couple millimeters of space between the top of the filling and top of the shell.

2. Return the molds to the refrigerator to chill for 30 minutes.

3. Once the ganache has chilled enough to feel firm to the touch, pour some more white candy melts on top to seal the ganache inside the duck. Pour enough candy melts to fill the mold. Return the mold to the refrigerator to chill for 1 to 2 hours, until the candy melts have fully set.

4. Unmold the ducks and set on a plate. Melt the black candy melts using the same technique you used to melt the white candy melts. Use a toothpick to draw the eyes and fangs on the ducks. Chill the ducks in the refrigerator for 10 minutes, then they are ready to serve!

To Serve:
1. Drop 1 or 2 ducks into a mug of warm milk and stir until you see the milk turn red. Then enjoy!

Pumpkin Spice Hot Chocolate

SERVES 2

A twist on the ever-popular pumpkin spice latte. Everything is better with chocolate, including the #PSL!

2 cups milk
½ cup cream
7 ounces good-quality milk chocolate
1 teaspoon pumpkin pie spice
¼ cup canned plain pumpkin
Whipped cream
Ground cinnamon, for topping

1. Place the milk, cream, chocolate, pumpkin pie spice, and canned pumpkin into a small pot and bring to a simmer. Heat until the chocolate has melted and everything is well combined.

2. Pour into mugs and top with whipped cream and a dusting of cinnamon. Enjoy!

Black Hot Chocolate

SERVES 2

This photo may look like it's in grayscale, but it's not!

1 cup good-quality milk chocolate

1½ cups milk

½ cup whipping cream

1 tablespoon activated charcoal powder, divided (see page 29 for more information)

1 tablespoon confectioners' sugar (optional)

2 cups whipping cream, whipped to soft peaks

1. Combine the chocolate, milk, whipping cream, and charcoal powder in a pot and set to medium heat. Stir constantly until the chocolate has fully melted and everything is well combined. Set aside.

2. Add the remaining charcoal powder and the confectioners' sugar, if using, to the whipped cream and beat with an electric mixer until stiff peaks form.

3. Place the cream in a piping bag fitted with a 2D or 6B piping tip.

4. Pour the hot chocolate into a glass and top with a swirl of whipped cream. Enjoy!

PUMPKIN SPICE MILKSHAKE

SERVES 1

I'm not ashamed to say that as soon as these photos were taken, this milkshake came into my living room with me and was eviscerated in mere minutes. It's so delicious, and I love that there is actual pumpkin inside. It works so well with the vanilla ice cream and the caramel drizzle.

1½ cups vanilla ice cream
¼ cup canned pure pumpkin
1 tablespoon pumpkin pie spice
½ cup cold milk
1 teaspoon vanilla extract
Caramel sauce
Whipped cream
Ground cinnamon
Cinnamon sticks

1. Place the ice cream, pumpkin, pumpkin pie spice, milk, and vanilla in a blender and pulse until smooth.

2. Squeeze the caramel sauce around the inside of your glass. Pour the milkshake into the glass and top with whipped cream, a dusting of ground cinnamon, and a cinnamon stick. Enjoy!

Spooky Milkshake

For an extra-fancy touch, add ¼ cup melted white chocolate when blending the ingredients together in step 1!

2½ cups vanilla ice cream
¾–1 cup milk
Dash of vanilla extract
Green and purple food coloring
Whipped cream
Green and black sprinkles
Salted Caramel Skull Truffles (page 87)

1. Divide the ice cream, milk, and vanilla into 3 equal portions. Pulse together ⅓ of the ice cream and milk at a time in a blender, adding a drop of either green or purple food coloring, or leaving it white. Repeat with the next ⅓ of the mixture, using the other color.

2. Layer the 3 colors in tall glasses. Using more milk will create a swirly pattern, while less milk will create more distinct lines between the colors.

3. Top with some whipped cream, sprinkles, and a Salted Caramel Skull Truffle and enjoy!

Eyeball Hot Chocolate

MAKES 2 SERVINGS OF HOT CHOCOLATE, WITH EXTRA MARSHMALLOWS

This hot chocolate is extra special because every element is homemade! This is a delicious, rich red velvet hot chocolate recipe topped with homemade eyeball marshmallows. Give the hot chocolate a stir to watch the eyeballs become bloodshot!

Marshmallows:

⅓ cup + ¼ cup cold water, divided

2½ teaspoons powdered gelatin

1 cup sugar

Blue food coloring

Chocolate chips

¼ cup confectioners' sugar

¼ cup cornstarch

Red Velvet Hot Chocolate:

2 cups milk

2 ounces dark, milk, or white chocolate, finely chopped

Red food coloring

Make the Marshmallows:

1. Pour ⅓ cup of cold water into the bowl of an electric mixer and sprinkle the powdered gelatin on top. Let sit for 5 minutes.

2. Place the sugar and ¼ cup water in a small pot and set to medium-high heat. Stir until the sugar has melted.

3. Attach a candy thermometer to the pot and boil the sugar until it reaches 238°F. Brush the sides of the pot with a wet pastry brush if sugar crystals stick to the sides.

4. Add the hot sugar to the gelatin and stir the mixture by hand, whisking for a few minutes to slightly cool. Then beat with an electric mixer on medium-high speed for 8 to 10 minutes, until soft peaks form.

5. Transfer the majority of the marshmallow to a piping bag fitted with a large, round piping tip. Dye the remaining marshmallow blue with a bit of food coloring and place in a piping bag fitted with a smaller round piping tip.

6. Line a baking sheet with parchment paper and pipe mounds with the white marshmallow. Stick the tip of the piping bag with the blue marshmallow slightly into the center of the white marshmallow and squeeze to create a blue center. Stick a chocolate chip pointy-side down into the center of the blue portion. Allow the marshmallows to set at room temperature for 1 to 2 hours, or until the surface is less sticky.

7. In a small bowl, combine the confectioners' sugar and cornstarch. Transfer to a sieve and dust over the marshmallows. Gently peel them off the parchment paper and dust the bottoms in the mixture as well. Place the marshmallows in the sieve and bounce a few times to remove any excess powder.

Make the Hot Chocolate:

1. Pour the milk into a small pot and set to medium heat. Add the chocolate and 2 to 3 drops red food coloring and stir until the chocolate has fully melted. Pour the hot chocolate into the mugs and top with the eyeballs. Enjoy!

SAVORY

Bone Crackers and Cauldron Dip

MAKES 2-3 CUPS

I'm not much of a dip person, but this is the exception! It's just fabulous. I baked it in a regular baking dish, then spooned it into this cute cauldron mug for serving.

1 sheet frozen puff pastry, defrosted
8 ounces cream cheese, room temperature
¼ cup sour cream
½ cup grated Parmesan cheese
1 garlic clove, finely chopped
½ teaspoon fresh basil, finely chopped
¼ teaspoon salt
Freshly ground pepper, to taste
½ cup frozen spinach, defrosted
14-ounce can artichoke hearts, drained and
   roughly chopped
¼ cup grated mozzarella cheese

Make the Crackers:

1. Preheat the oven to 400°F and line a baking sheet with parchment paper.

2. Place the sheet of puff pastry onto a floured work surface. Use a bone-shaped cookie cutter to cut out bone shapes. They can be any size you like!

3. Place the crackers onto your prepared baking sheet, and place another sheet of parchment paper on top, then another baking sheet. The weight of the second baking sheet will keep the puff pastry from puffing up and create flat crackers, perfect for dipping!

4. Bake for 10 to 15 minutes, until the crackers are golden brown. Cool the crackers completely.

Make the Dip:

1. Preheat the oven to 350°F or lower the temperature if you're doing this right after the crackers.

2. Place the cream cheese, sour cream, Parmesan cheese, garlic, basil, salt, and pepper in a bowl and beat with an electric mixer until smooth.

3. Wrap the frozen spinach in a paper towel and squeeze until all the excess water has drained away. Add the spinach to the mixture, along with the artichoke hearts and mozzarella cheese. Mix well.

4. Pour the dip into a small baking dish and bake for 25 minutes, until the top is slightly browned.

5. Cool slightly, then serve!

GHOSTLY SESAME CROSTINI

MAKES 5 CROSTINI

Theses spooky little crostini are topped with homemade black sesame spread, which is a fun alternative to the also dark and spooky olive spread. Olive haters—I know you're out there in masses—this is for you!

7 tablespoons toasted black sesame seeds
1½ tablespoons sesame oil
1½ tablespoons honey
2 pinches of salt
⅓ baguette
¼ ball of fresh mozzarella cheese
1 sheet of nori seaweed

1. First, make the sesame seed paste. Place the sesame seeds in a food processor and pulse until they are finely ground and are secreting their oil. Then add the sesame oil, honey, and salt, and mix. This will make enough for about 15 crostini.

2. Slice the baguette into long, oval slices, and toast. Then slice the mozzarella into oval slices.

3. Spread the sesame seed paste onto the toast, then place the mozzarella slices on top. Slice eye, face, or mask markings out of the nori, and stick them directly onto the cheese.

CREEPY CHEESE BALLS

EACH VARIATION MAKES ABOUT 4 CUPS CHEESE MIX

These cheese balls will shock and amuse your guests! My poor family was subject to these on Canadian Thanksgiving, as I'd just finished shooting this recipe, and had so much fun discovering the flavors and telling me that they "loved the brain!" I am a sucker for goat cheese, so variation 3 is my go-to option, but the fresh apple in variation 1 tastes spectacular. Looking for a more traditional flavor? Try variation 2!

Prosciutto

Variation 1:
1 cup chopped red apple
1 cup chopped green apple
16 ounces cream cheese, room temperature
1½ cups grated orange cheddar cheese
1½ teaspoon maple syrup
1½ cups pecans, finely chopped

Variation 2:
16 ounces cream cheese, room temperature
2 cups grated orange cheddar cheese
1 tablespoon Dijon mustard
Pinch of black pepper
1 cup pecans, finely chopped

Variation 3:
16 ounces cream cheese, room temperature
1 cup grated cheddar cheese (white and
   orange mix)
1 cup goat cheese, room temperature
Pinch of black pepper

1. Mix all the ingredients for whichever variation you prefer.

2. Line a skull-, brain-, or heart-shaped mold with prosciutto. Allow the excess to hang off the edges. Press the prosciutto into as many crevices of the mold as possible.

3. Fill the molds with the cheese mixture, pressing it firmly into the mold. Fold the excess prosciutto on top of the cheese and smooth the surface.

4. Cover with plastic wrap and place something heavy on top, like a large can. Place the mold in the refrigerator and chill overnight.

5. Carefully unmold the cheese balls and serve with crackers!

Skull Calzones

MAKES 6 MEDIUM-SIZE CALZONES

Calzones may sound intimidating, but all you need is some pizza dough and a spooky skull cake pan!

Cooking spray
24 ounces pizza dough
1 large egg
1 teaspoon water

Margherita Filling (per calzone):
2 tablespoons pizza sauce
1 (½-inch) cube mozzarella
2 fresh basil leaves, roughly torn

Dessert Filling (per calzone):
2 tablespoons chocolate hazelnut spread
2 banana slices
1 strawberry, halved
2 raspberries
3 mini marshmallows

1. Preheat oven to 375°F and spray a skull baking tin with cooking spray.

2. Roll out the pizza dough until it is about ¼-inch thick, then cut into 6 rectangles. Working with one rectangle of dough at a time, drape it into the baking tin and fill with your desired filling. Fold the edges of the dough together and pinch to seal closed.

3. In a small bowl, beat the egg and water, then brush onto the surface of the dough. Place the baking tin in the refrigerator for 30 minutes, then bake for 18 to 20 minutes, until the crust is golden brown.

4. Remove from the pan and enjoy!

Skeleton Hair Pasta with Homemade Pesto

SERVES 4

My boyfriend is from Genoa, Italy, which is the center for all things pesto in Italy. I was lucky enough to have him as my guide for this recipe, so you know it's going to be amazing! I recommend using organic basil as it tastes so much more vibrant.

½ cup pine nuts

5 cups fresh basil leaves

1 clove garlic, peeled

½ cup grated Parmesan cheese, plus extra for garnishing

¼ cup grated pecorino Romano cheese

¼ teaspoon salt, plus large pinch for pasta water

¾ cup good-quality extra-virgin olive oil, plus extra for garnishing

18 ounces squid ink spaghetti

1. First, make the pesto. Place the pine nuts, basil, garlic, Parmesan, pecorino, and salt in a blender or food processor and pulse until you create a paste.

2. Gradually add the olive oil about 2 tablespoons at a time, pulsing with each addition. Set aside.

3. Fill a large pot with water and add a large pinch of salt. Set to high heat and bring to a boil. Add the spaghetti and cook according to instructions on the package.

4. Drain the spaghetti and toss with the pesto. Serve with an additional sprinkle of Parmesan cheese and drizzle of olive oil.

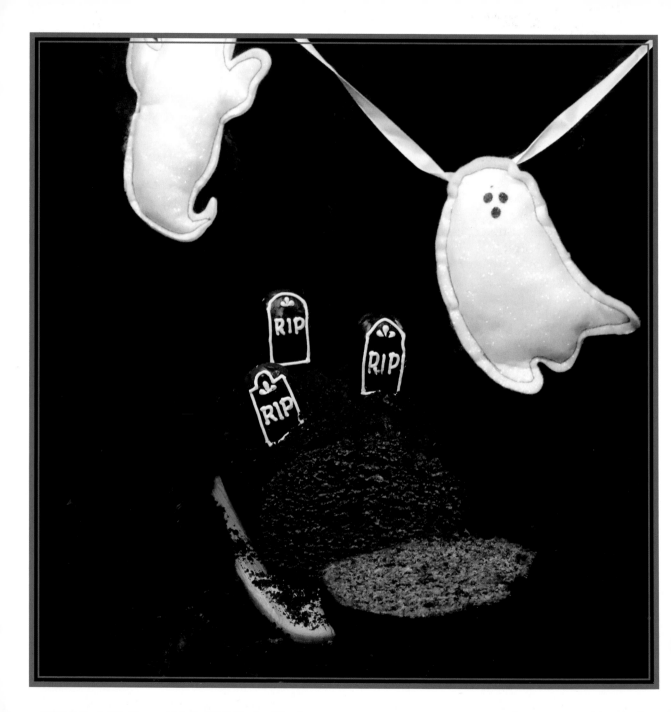

GRAVEYARD BANANA BREAD

MAKES 1 LOAF

This banana bread recipe has been passed down from my mom to me, as she filled my childhood with banana bread and muffins. It's not too sweet, so it can be eaten as a treat for breakfast. We're making it a little sweeter today with the addition of chocolate sandwich cookies, which give it a deep, spooky look! When pulsing the cookies, don't remove the cream filling! It add an even more decadent flavor to the banana bread.

3 ripe bananas, mashed

6 tablespoons vegetable oil (olive oil is fine, or canola if you have it)

½ cup sugar

1 egg

1 teaspoon vanilla extract

¼ teaspoon salt

1½ cups all-purpose flour

1 teaspoon baking soda

1 teaspoon baking powder

12 chocolate sandwich cookies

2 ladyfingers

½ cup black candy melts

½ cup vanilla buttercream (page 3)

1. Preheat oven to 350°F and spray a loaf pan with cooking spray.

2. Combine bananas, oil, and sugar. Then add the egg, vanilla, and salt.

3. Mix flour, baking soda, and baking powder in a separate bowl and add to banana mixture.

4. Place the cookies in a food processor and pulse until they become a fine crumb. Fold ¾ of the crumbs into the banana bread.

5. Pour the batter into your prepared pan and smooth the surface. Sprinkle the remaining cookie crumbs on top.

6. Bake for about 45 minutes, or until a knife inserted into the center of the loaf comes out clean. Cool completely.

7. Use a sharp knife to cut the ladyfingers in half. Set aside.

8. Place the black candy melts into a microwave-safe bowl. Microwave for 30-second intervals until melted, stirring at each interval.

9. Dunk each rounded half of the ladyfingers (4 total) into the black candy melts. Place them on a plate lined with a sheet of parchment paper, then transfer the plate to the refrigerator to chill until the candy melts have set.

10. Place the buttercream into a piping bag fitted with a small, round piping tip. Once the candy melts have hardened, pipe gravestone details onto the ladyfingers.

11. Use a sharp knife to slice little slots into the top of the banana bread. Insert the ladyfingers into the slots to look like upright tombstones.

12. Slice and enjoy!

Pumpkin Latte Breakfast Skulls

MAKES 6 SKULL CAKES

My trusty skull cakelette pan comes in handy for another recipe in this book! These breakfast skulls are great eaten as is, but can also be sliced, toasted, and topped with butter. You will thank me, I promise!

Cooking spray
2 large eggs
1½ cups sugar
1½ cups plain canned pumpkin puree (not fresh puree—it gets too runny)
½ cup unsalted butter, melted
2 tablespoons powdered instant coffee
2½ cups all-purpose flour
2 teaspoons baking soda
½ teaspoon salt
1½ teaspoons cinnamon
¾ teaspoon ground ginger
½ teaspoon ground nutmeg
⅛ teaspoon allspice
⅛ teaspoon ground cloves

1. Preheat oven to 350°F and spray a skull pan with cooking spray.

2. Whisk together the eggs, sugar, pumpkin puree, butter, and instant coffee in a large bowl. In a separate bowl, mix the flour, baking soda, salt, cinnamon, ginger, nutmeg, allspice, and cloves, then add to the pumpkin mixture and mix together.

3. Divide the batter into your prepared pan and bake for 30 to 35 minutes until fully cooked. Allow it to cool for 15 minutes in the pan, then remove from the pan and cool completely on a cooling rack.

SEA WITCH RISOTTO

SERVES 4

I was lucky enough to wrangle in my Italian boyfriend's talents for another recipe in this book—risotto! It can feel laborious because you have to slowly ladle in stock and stir constantly, but the result is a restaurant-quality dish that looks so cool and spooky! Are you brave enough to face the sea witch?

4 cups vegetable, chicken, or fish stock

3 tablespoons extra-virgin olive oil, divided

½ medium onion, diced

1 clove garlic, finely diced

½ cup white wine, divided

½ cup frozen green peas, defrosted

1 cup arborio rice

1 tablespoon squid ink

5 ounces cooked octopus tentacles

7 ounces cleaned squid cut into rings, with tentacles

Parsley, for garnish

1. Pour the stock into a pot and set to medium heat. Keep the stock on the heat and warm during the entire cooking process. If it comes to a boil, reduce the heat to just a simmer.

2. In a separate pan, add 1 tablespoon olive oil and the onion and garlic. Cook on medium heat until the onion is translucent and fragrant. Add 1 tablespoon white wine and continue cooking for another 3 minutes.

3. Add the green peas and cook for an additional 2 to 3 minutes. If desired, reserve some peas for garnishing, as they will darken once the squid ink is added.

4. Add the rice and sauté for 2 to 3 minutes, stirring constantly. Add 1 ladle of stock while continuously stirring. Once the stock has been absorbed by the rice, add another ladle. Continue until you have used up half of the stock.

5. Add the squid ink and stir to combine. Continue to add the rest of the stock, waiting until the previous addition is completely absorbed each time, until the rice reaches your desired softness. You may not need to use all of the stock.

6. While the rice is cooking, place the octopus in a separate pan with 1 tablespoon olive oil. Set to medium-high heat and cook until warmed through. Transfer to a plate and set aside. Place the squid in the pan, along with the last tablespoon of olive oil and the remaining white wine. Cook on medium-high heat until the squid is opaque and fully cooked through, about 3 to 5 minutes.

7. Add the squid to the risotto and mix well.

8. Spoon the risotto onto plates. Top with the octopus tentacles, reserved green peas, and some parsley.

Haunted Mansion Loaf

MAKES A 6-INCH TALL HOUSE

The mansion portion of this loaf is actually a tomato soup cake! It sounds a little scary, but it surprisingly doesn't taste of tomatoes, despite using 2 cans! It tastes like fall—spiced and warm. Then slice into this mansion to discover the ghosts inside!

Ghosts:

1 cup unsalted butter, room temperature

2 cups sugar

3 teaspoons vanilla extract

6 large eggs

3 cups all-purpose flour

1 teaspoon baking soda

1 teaspoon salt

1½ cups sour cream

Haunted Mansion:

20 ounces tomato soup

2 teaspoons baking soda

2 cups sugar

1 cup unsalted butter, room temperature

4 cups all-purpose flour

4 teaspoons baking powder

2 teaspoons cinnamon

2 teaspoons nutmeg

1 teaspoon cloves

3 tablespoons confectioners' sugar, for dusting

Make the Ghosts:

1. Preheat oven to 350°F and grease and flour a 10×15-inch Swiss roll pan.

2. Beat the butter and sugar with an electric mixer until pale and smooth. Add the vanilla and eggs, one at a time, mixing with each addition.

3. In a separate bowl, combine the flour, baking soda, and salt. Add this to the batter in 2 additions, alternating with the sour cream.

4. Spoon the batter into your prepared pan and bake for 30 to 40 minutes, or until a skewer inserted into the center comes out clean. Cool completely.

5. Use a serrated knife to slice off the top and bottom browned portions of the cake.

6. Cut out ghosts with a ghost cookie cutter. Set aside.

Make the Mansion:

1. Preheat the oven to 350°F (or keep it on if you're baking directly after making the ghost portion) and grease and flour a house-shaped cake mold pan.

2. Pour the tomato soup into a bowl. Add the baking soda and mix until fully combined. It may foam up, but that's normal!

3. Place the sugar and butter in a bowl and beat with an electric mixer until pale and fluffy. Then add the soup mixture and combine.

(Continued on next page)

4. In a separate bowl, combine the flour, baking powder, cinnamon, nutmeg, and cloves, then add to the butter mixture and mix until fully combined.

5. Spoon about ⅓ of the batter into your prepared house pan. Stick the ghosts vertically into the pan, making sure that they are touching each other and their "bottoms" are facing up. Make a mark with cake batter on the outside of the cake pan to note which way the ghosts are facing. This will be important when you slice the cake—you want to make sure the ghosts are positioned correctly in the slices! Pour the remaining mixture around the ghosts, so that they are "floating" in the batter.

6. Bake the cake for at least 60 minutes, until a knife inserted into the cake comes out clean. Be sure to stick the knife into all areas where the tomato cake is—on top and to the sides of the ghosts. If you find that the cake is browning too quickly, simply place a sheet of aluminum foil on top.

7. Once the cake is fully cooked, transfer it to a wire rack and cool it while still in the pan.

8. Use a serrated knife to trim off the base of the cake so that it sits flat. It's handy to do this while the cake is still in the pan, as the house can be a tricky shape to get a hold of.

9. Place the house on your desired serving tray. Place some confectioners' sugar in a mesh sieve and gently dust over to highlight the features of the cake.

10. Slice and enjoy your spooky surprise!

Eyeballs and Meat Sauce

SERVES 2

This meat sauce is a favorite of mine. It does take some time to make, but it's absolutely worth it. It also pairs wonderfully well with spaghetti for a Bolognese-style dish. The eyeball dumplings are homemade mochi, with the addition of fresh Parmesan cheese and salt and pepper, for a more savory flavor.

Sauce:
1 slice bacon
1½ tablespoons olive oil
¼ cup diced onion
¼ cup diced carrot
¼ cup diced celery
1 clove garlic, minced
10 ounces ground beef
½ cup red wine
2 tablespoons tomato paste
7 ounces canned chopped tomatoes
2 cups chicken stock
1 bay leaf
A pinch each of salt, pepper, and sugar

Eyeball Dumplings:
2 ounces shiratamako rice flour (plus extra if needed)
3 tablespoons grated Parmesan cheese
Salt and pepper
¾ cup water
Blue, green, and brown food coloring

For the Sauce:

1. Finely chop the bacon, then drizzle the olive oil into a pot set to medium heat. Add the bacon, onion, carrot, celery, and garlic, and cook until the onions become translucent.

2. Add the ground beef and increase the heat to high. Once the meat has browned on the surface, add the red wine and allow it to fully reduce.

3. Add the tomato paste and combine well. Then add the canned tomatoes, the chicken stock, and the bay leaf, then reduce to medium heat and cook for 40 minutes until it is reduced by half, mixing occasionally.

4. Once it has reduced by half, remove the bay leaf, season with salt, pepper, and a bit of sugar to taste.

For the Dumplings:

1. Place the shiratamako flour into a bowl, and mix in the Parmesan cheese and salt and pepper.

2. Gradually drizzle in the water, and knead with a spoon (or your hands, which is much easier). The dough should form into one piece, and be firm enough for a piece of dough to be rolled into a ball, and retain its form when placed down. Depending on the humidity of your house and the moisture in the cheese, you may need to add more flour, but do so gradually.

(Continued on page 195)

3. Divide the dough into about 48 pieces, and roll into balls. Take 3 balls and knead 1 together with a few drops of blue food coloring, one with the green, and one with the brown to create 1 blue, 1 green, and 1 brown ball. Take a small amount of dough from the blue or green dough, flatten it into a disk, and stick it onto one of the white balls. Then take an even smaller amount of brown dough and stick it on top to make the pupil. Repeat with the remaining eyeballs.

4. Place the dumplings in a pot of salted, boiling water. Once they have risen to the surface, boil for 1 minute, then place them into the pot with the meat sauce. Gently mix, and serve!

Skull Calzones, page 181

Acknowledgments

First and foremost, I want to thank *you*! Thank you so much for picking up my book and taking an interest in my recipes. Whether this is the first time we're "meeting" or if you've been following me for a while, I want you to know how much I appreciate your support. I would not be where I am today, living my dream, without each and every like, comment, and follow. I hope this book has been everything you hoped it would be. If you have any questions about the recipes in this book, or any recipe of mine, send me a message on social media and I'll be happy to help you!

I also want to thank my amazing editor, Leah Zarra. She has been my editor for all five of my books and has done such an amazing job transforming my recipes from manuscripts into beautiful, sparkling books! She has developed the ability to read my mind and turns my confusing, inarticulate recipe descriptions into funny, charming little blurbs with jokes that actually make sense. This book wouldn't be in your hands without her!

Last, but certainly not least, I'd like to thank my amazing boyfriend, Marco. He helped to develop several of the savory recipes in this book and was the official taste tester for all the rest! He was also so patient and supportive of me taking over our entire kitchen and living room while shooting this book, never once complaining about the hoards of Halloween decorations and filming equipment piled on every surface well past spooky season.

Cauldron Cupcakes with Gooey Centers, page 3

INDEX

nutmeg
Caramel Apple Cake Pops, 71–73
DIY Pumpkin Spice Mix, 101
Haunted Mansion Loaf, 191–192
Pumpkin Latte Breakfast Skulls, 187
Pumpkin Spice Cupcakes, 9
Shrunken Head Apple Cider, 157

O

onions
Eyeballs and Meat Sauce, 193–195
orange
Shrunken Head Apple Cider, 157
orange juice
Blood Bag Drinks, 159
Oreos
Worm Cheesecake, 65–67
Ouija Board Sheet Cake, 45–46

P

panna cotta
Bleeding Heart Panna Cotta, 115
pasta
Skeleton Hair Pasta with Homemade
Pesto, 183
pastry, puff
Bone Crackers and Cauldron Dip, 175
peanut butter
Glowing Ghosts Cake, 31–32
peanut butter chips
Bloody PB&J Cups, 141–142
pearl dust
Sparkling Unicorn Blood, 151
peas
Sea Witch Risotto, 189
pecans
Creepy Cheese Balls, 179
pesto
Skeleton Hair Pasta with Homemade
Pesto, 183
Petri Dish Treats, 127
pie
Mini Pumpkin Pie Gravestones, 81

pine nuts
Skeleton Hair Pasta with Homemade
Pesto, 183
Pink Lemonade Halloween Cake, 41–43
Pocky
Haunted House Cake, 53–55
Poison Apple Cake, 23–24
pomegranate juice
Bleeding Cake, 33–35
pudding
Brain Pudding, 117
Toad Eye Pudding, 125
pumpkin
Chocolate Pumpkin Cupcakes, 11
Mini Pumpkin Pie Gravestones, 81
Pumpkin Bundt Cake, 63–64
Pumpkin Dumplings, 123
Pumpkin Latte Breakfast Skulls, 187
Pumpkin Spice Hot Chocolate, 163
Pumpkin Spice Milkshake, 167
Pumpkin Bundt Cake, 63–64
Pumpkin Cake Pops, 75
Chocolate Pumpkin Cupcakes, 11
Pumpkin Dumplings, 123
Pumpkin Juice, 145
Pumpkin Latte Breakfast Skulls, 187
pumpkin pie spice
Candy Corn Cake, 51–52
Mini Pumpkin Pie Gravestones, 81
pumpkins, candy
Pumpkin Spice Cupcakes, 9
pumpkin spice
DIY Pumpkin Spice Mix, 101
Pumpkin Bundt Cake, 63–64
Pumpkin Spice Milkshake, 167
Pumpkin Spice Cupcakes, 9
Pumpkin Spice Hot Chocolate, 163
Pumpkin Spice Milkshake, 167

R

Rainbow Candy Apples, 137
raisins
Haunted House Cake, 53–55
Slithering Snake Cupcakes, 15–17

raspberries
Red Blood Cell Dumplings, 111
Rose Gold Skull Cake, 47–49
Skull Calzones, 181
Sparkling Unicorn Blood, 151
raspberry jam
Bleeding Cake, 33–35
Bloody PB&J Cups, 141–142
Vampire Duck Hot Chocolate Bombs,
161
Red Blood Cell Dumplings, 111
rice
Sea Witch Risotto, 189
Rose Gold Skull Cake, 47–49

S

Salted Caramel Skull Truffles, 87
Spooky Milkshake, 169
seaweed
Ghostly Sesame Crostini, 177
Sea Witch Risotto, 189
Shrunken Head Apple Cider, 157
Skeleton Hair Pasta with Homemade
Pesto, 183
Skeleton Macarons, 79
Skull Cakes with Gooey Brains, 37
Skull Calzones, 181
skull candy
Cauldron Cupcakes with Gooey
Centers, 3
Slithering Snake Cupcakes, 15–17
soda
cream
Pumpkin Juice, 145
Sparkling Unicorn Blood, 151
ginger ale
Pumpkin Juice, 145
Sprite
Magical Potion, 149
Specimen Jar Drinks, 153
water
Specimen Jar Drinks, 153
sour cream
Bone Crackers and Cauldron Dip, 175

Conversion Charts

Metric and Imperial Conversions

(These conversions are rounded for convenience)

Ingredient	Cups/Tablespoons/Teaspoons	Ounces	Grams/Milliliters
Butter	1 cup/ 16 tablespoons/2 sticks	8 ounces	230 grams
Cheese, shredded	1 cup	4 ounces	110 grams
Cream cheese	1 tablespoon	0.5 ounce	14.5 grams
Cornstarch	1 tablespoon	0.3 ounce	8 grams
Flour, all-purpose	1 cup/1 tablespoon	4.5 ounces/0.3 ounce	125 grams/8 grams
Flour, whole wheat	1 cup	4 ounces	120 grams
Fruit, dried	1 cup	4 ounces	120 grams
Fruits or veggies, chopped	1 cup	5 to 7 ounces	145 to 200 grams
Fruits or veggies, pureed	1 cup	8.5 ounces	245 grams
Honey, maple syrup, or corn syrup	1 tablespoon	0.75 ounce	20 grams
Liquids: cream, milk, water, or juice	1 cup	8 fluid ounces	240 milliliters
Oats	1 cup	5.5 ounces	150 grams
Salt	1 teaspoon	0.2 ounce	6 grams
Spices: cinnamon, cloves, ginger, or nutmeg (ground)	1 teaspoon	0.2 ounce	5 milliliters
Sugar, brown, firmly packed	1 cup	7 ounces	200 grams
Sugar, white	1 cup/1 tablespoon	7 ounces/0.5 ounce	200 grams/12.5 grams
Vanilla extract	1 teaspoon	0.2 ounce	4 grams

Oven Temperatures

Fahrenheit	Celsius	Gas Mark
225°	110°	¼
250°	120°	½
275°	140°	1
300°	150°	2
325°	160°	3
350°	180°	4
375°	190°	5
400°	200°	6
425°	220°	7
450°	230°	8

ALSO AVAILABLE

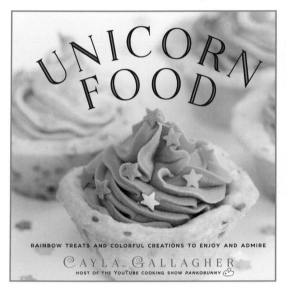

UNICORN FOOD

RAINBOW TREATS AND COLORFUL CREATIONS TO ENJOY AND ADMIRE

CAYLA GALLAGHER

HOST OF THE YouTube COOKING SHOW *PANKOBUNNY*

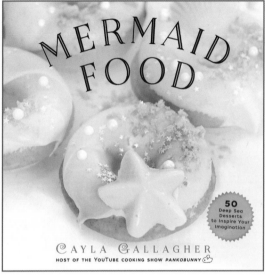

MERMAID FOOD

50 Deep Sea Desserts to Inspire Your Imagination

CAYLA GALLAGHER

HOST OF THE YouTube COOKING SHOW *PANKOBUNNY*

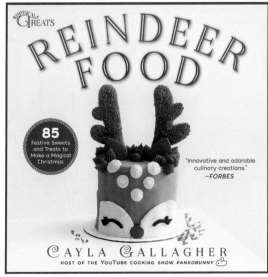

WHIMSICAL TREATS

REINDEER FOOD

85 Festive Sweets and Treats to Make a Magical Christmas

"Innovative and adorable culinary creations."
~FORBES

CAYLA GALLAGHER

HOST OF THE YouTube COOKING SHOW *PANKOBUNNY*